SHELBURNE ESSAYS

FIRST SERIES

Shelburne Essays

FIRST SERIES

By Paul Elmer More

" Before we have an American literature,
we must have an American criticism."
— J. R. LOWELL.

PHAETON PRESS

NEW YORK   MCMLXVII

Originally Published 1904
Reprinted 1967

Published by Phaeton Press, Inc.
By arrangement with Mrs. Harry B. Fine

Library of Congress Catalog Card Number 67-17764

Printed in U.S.A.
EDWARDS BROTHERS, INC.
Ann Arbor, Michigan

CONTENTS

SHELBURNE ESSAYS

——

A HERMIT'S NOTES ON THOREAU

NEAR the secluded village of Shelburne that
lies along the peaceful valley of the Androscoggin,
I took upon myself to live two years as a hermit
after a mild Epicurean fashion of my own.   Three
maiden aunts wagged their heads ominously; my
nearest friend inquired cautiously whether there
was any taint of insanity in the family; an old
grey-haired lady, a veritable saint who had not
been soured by her many deeds of charity, admon-
ished me on the utter selfishness and godlessness
of such a proceeding.   But I clung heroically to
my resolution.   Summer tourists in that pleasant
valley may still see the little red house among the
pines,—empty now, I believe; and I dare say
gaudy coaches still draw up at the door, as they
used to do, when the gaudier bonnets and hats
exchanged wondering remarks on the cabalistic
inscription over the lintel, or spoke condescend-
ingly to the great dog lying on the steps.   As for
the hermit within, having found it impossible to

educe any meaning from the tangled habits of mankind while he himself was whirled about in the imbroglio, he had determined to try the efficacy of undisturbed meditation at a distance. So deficient had been his education that he was actually better acquainted with the aspirations and emotions of the old dwellers on the Ganges than with those of the modern toilers by the Hudson or the Potomac. He had been deafened by the "indistinguishable roar" of the streets, and could make no sense of the noisy jargon of the market place. But—shall it be confessed?— although he discovered many things during his contemplative sojourn in the wilderness, and learned that the attempt to criticise and not to create literature was to be his labour in this world, nevertheless he returned to civilisation as ignorant, alas, of its meaning as when he left it.

However, it is not my intention to justify the saintly old lady's charge of egotism by telling the story of my exodus to the desert; that, perhaps, may come later and at a more suitable time. I wish now only to record the memories of one perfect day in June, when woods and mountains were as yet a new delight.

The fresh odours of morning were still swaying in the air when I set out on this particular day; and my steps turned instinctively to the great pine forest, called the Cathedral Woods, that filled the valley and climbed the hill slopes behind my house. There, many long roads that are laid

down in no map wind hither and thither among
the trees, whose leafless trunks tower into the
sky and then meet in evergreen arches overhead.
There,

The tumult of the times disconsolate

never enters, and no noise of the world is heard
save now and then, in winter, the ringing strokes
of the woodchopper at his cruel task.   How many
times I have walked those quiet cathedral aisles,
while my great dog paced faithfully on before!
Underfoot the dry, purple-hued moss was stretched
like a royal carpet; and at intervals a glimpse of
the deep sky, caught through an aperture in the
groined roof, reminded me of the other world,
and carried my thoughts still farther from the
desolating memories of this life.   Nothing but
pure odours were there, sweeter than cloistral incense; and murmurous voices of the pines, more
harmonious than the chanting of trained choris-
ters; and in the heart of the wanderer nothing
but tranquillity and passionless peace.

Often now the recollection of those scenes comes
floating back upon his senses when, in the wake-
ful seasons of a summer night, he hears the wind
at work among the trees; even in barren city
streets some sound or spectacle can act upon him
as a spell, banishing for a moment the hideous
contention of commerce, and placing him beneath
the restful shadows of the pines.   May his understanding cease its function, and his heart forget to
feel, when the memory of those days has utterly

left him and he walks in the world without this
consolation of remembered peace.

Nor can I recollect that my mind, in these
walks, was much called away from contemplation
by the petty curiosities of the herbalist or bird-
lorist, for I am not one zealously addicted to
scrutinising into the minuter secrets of Nature. It
never seemed to me that a flower was made sweeter
by knowing the construction of its ovaries, or assumed a new importance when I learned its trivial
or scientific name. The wood thrush and the
veery sing as melodiously to the uninformed as to
the subtly curious. Indeed, I sometimes think a
little ignorance is wholesome in our communion
with Nature, until we are ready to part with her
altogether. She is feminine in this as in other
respects, and loves to shroud herself in illusions,
as the Hindus taught in their books. For they
called her Mâyâ, the very person and power of
deception, whose sway over the beholder must
end as soon as her mystery is penetrated.

Dear as the sound of the wood thrush's note
still is to my ears, something of charm and allurement has gone from it since I have become intimate with the name and habits of the bird. As
a child born and reared in the city, that wild,
ringing call was perfectly new and strange to me
when, one early dawn, I first heard it during a
visit to the Delaware Water Gap. To me, whose
ears had grown familiar only with the rumble of
paved streets, the sound was like a reiterated un-

earthly summons inviting me from my narrow prison existence out into a wide and unexplored world of impulse and adventure. Long afterwards I learned the name of the songster whose note had made so strong an impression on my childish senses, but still I associate the song with the grandiose scenery, with the sheer forests and streams and the rapid river of the Water Gap. I was indeed almost a man—though the confession may sound incredible in these days—before I again heard the wood thrush's note, and my second adventure impressed me almost as profoundly as the first. In the outer suburbs of the city where my home had always been, I was walking one day with a brother, when suddenly out of a grove of laurel oaks sounded, clear and triumphant, the note which I remembered so well, but which had come to have to my imagination the unreality and mystery of a dream of long ago. Instantly my heart leapt within me. "It is the fateful summons once more!" I cried; and, with my companion who was equally ignorant of bird-lore, I ran into the grove to discover the wild trumpeter. That was a strange chase in the fading twilight, while the unknown songster led us on from tree to tree, ever deeper into the woods. Many times we saw him on one of the lower boughs, but could not for a long while bring ourselves to believe that so wondrous a melody should proceed from so plain a minstrel. And at last, when we had satisfied ourselves of his identity, and the night

had fallen, we came out into the road with a
strange solemnity hanging over us.   Our ears had
been opened to the unceasing harmonies of creation, and our eyes had been made aware of the
endless drama of natural life.   We had been
initiated into the lesser mysteries;   and if the
sacred pageantry was not then, and never was
to be, perfectly clear to our understanding, the
imagination was nevertheless awed and purified.

If the knowledge and experience of years have
made me a little more callous to these deeper influences, at least I have not deliberately closed
the door to them by incautious prying.   Perhaps
a long course of wayward reading has taught me
to look upon the world with eyes quite different
from those of the modern exquisite searchers into
Nature.   I remember the story of Prometheus,
and think his punishment is typical of the penalty
that falls upon those who grasp at powers and
knowledge not intended for mankind,— some
nemesis of a more material loneliness and a more
barren pride torturing them because they have
turned from human knowledge to an alien and
forbidden sphere.   Like Prometheus, they shall
in the end cry out in vain:—

> O air divine, and O swift-wingëd winds!
> Ye river fountains, and thou myriad-twinkling
> Laughter of ocean waves!   O mother earth!
> And thou, O all-discerning orb o' the sun!—
> To you, I cry to you ; behold what I,
> A god, endure of evil from the gods.

Nor is the tale of Prometheus alone in teaching
this lesson of prudence, nor was Greece the only
land of antiquity where reverence was deemed
more salutary than curiosity. The myth of the
veiled Isis passed in those days from people to
people, and was everywhere received as a symbol
of the veil of illusion about Nature, which no man
might lift with impunity. And the same idea
was, if anything, intensified in the Middle Ages.
The common people, and the Church as well,
looked with horror on such scholars as Pope
Gerbert, who was thought, for his knowledge of
Nature, to have sold himself to the devil; and on
such discoverers as Roger Bacon, whose wicked
searching into forbidden things cost him fourteen
years in prison. And even in modern times did
not the poet Blake say: " I fear Wordsworth loves
nature, and nature is the work of the Devil. The
Devil is in us as far as we are nature"? It has
remained for an age of scepticism to substitute
investigation for awe. After all, can any course
of study or open-air pedagogics bring us into real
communion with the world about us? I fear
much of the talk about companionship with Nature that pervades our summer life is little better
than cant and self-deception, and he best understands the veiled goddess who most frankly admits
her impenetrable secrecy. The peace that comes
to us from contemplating the vast panorama spread
out before us is due rather to the sense of a great
passionless power entirely out of our domain than

to any real intimacy with the hidden deity. It
was John Woolman, the famous New Jersey
Quaker, who wrote, during a journey through
the wilderness of Pennsylvania: "In my travelling on the road, I often felt a cry rise from the
centre of my mind, thus, 'O Lord, I am a stranger
on the earth, hide not thy face from me.'"

But I forget that I am myself travelling on the
road; and all this long disquisition is only a chapter of reminiscences, due to the multitudinous
singing of the thrushes on this side and that, as
we—I and my great dog—trod the high cathedral
aisles. After a while the sound of running water
came to us above the deeper diapason of the pines,
and, turning aside, we clambered down to a brook
which we had already learned to make the ter-
minus of our walks. Along this stream we had
discovered a dozen secret nooks where man and
dog might lie or sit at ease, and to-day I stretched
myself on a cool, hollow rock, with my eyes looking up the long, leafy chasm of the brook. Just
above my couch the current was dammed by a
row of mossy boulders, over which the waters
poured with a continual murmur and plash. My
head was only a little higher than the pool beyond
the boulders, and, lying motionless, I watched the
flies weaving a pattern over the surface of the
quiet water, and now and then was rewarded by
seeing a greedy trout leap into the sunlight to
capture one of the winged weavers. Surely, if
there is any such thing as real intimacy with

Nature, it is in just such secluded spots as this;
for the grander scenes require of us a moral enthusiasm which can come to the soul only at rare
intervals and for brief moments. From these
chosen mountain retreats, one might send to a
scientist, busy with his books and instruments
and curious to pry into the secret powers of Nature, some such an appeal as this:—

Brother, awhile your impious engines leave ;
  Nor always seek with flame-compelling wires
Out of the palsied hand of Zeus to reave
  His dear celestial fires.

What though he drowse upon a tottering bench,
  Forgetful how his random bolts are hurled !
Are you to blame ? or is it yours to quench
  The thunders of the world?

Come learn with me through folly to be wise :
  Think you by cunning laws of optic lore
To lend the enamelled fields or burning skies
  One splendour lacked before?

A wizard footrule to the waves of sound
  You lay,—hath measure in the song of bird
Or ever in the voice of waters found
  One melody erst unheard ?

Ah, for a season close your magic books,
  Your rods and crystals in the closet hide ;
I know in covert ways a hundred nooks,
  High on the mountain side,

Where through the golden hours that follow noon,
    Under the greenwood shadows you and I
May talk of happy lives, until too soon
    Night's shadows fold the sky.

And while like incense blown among the leaves
    Our fragrant smoke ascends from carven bowl,
We'll con the lesser wisdom that deceives
    The Questioner in the soul,

And laugh to hoodwink where we cannot rout:—
    Did Bruno of the stubborn heart outbrave,
Or could the mind of Galileo flout
    The folly of the Grave?

So it seemed to me that the lesser wisdom of
quiet content before the face of Nature's mysteries
might be studied in the untrained garden of my
hermitage.   But I have been dreaming and moral-
ising on the little life about me and the greater
life of the world too long.   So lying near the level
of the still pool I began to read.   The volume
chosen was the most appropriate to the time
and place that could be imagined,—Thoreau's
Walden; and having entered upon an experiment
not altogether unlike his, I now set myself to
reading the record of his two years of solitude.
I learned many things from that morning's perusal.   Several times I had read the *Odyssey* within
sight of the sea; and the murmur of the waves
on the beach, beating through the rhythm of the
poem, had taught me how vital a thing a book
might be, and how it could acquire a peculiar

validity from harmonious surroundings; but now
the reading of Thoreau in that charmed and lonely
spot emphasised this commonplace truth in a
special manner. *Walden* studied in the closet,
and *Walden* mused over under the trees, by running water, are two quite different books. And
then, from Thoreau, the greatest by far of our
writers on Nature, and the creator of a new sentiment in literature, my mind turned to the long list
of Americans who have left, or are still composing,
a worthy record of their love and appreciation of
the natural world. Our land of multiform activities has produced so little that is really creative
in literature or art! Hawthorne and Poe, and
possibly one or two others, were masters in their
own field; yet even they chose not quite the highest realm for their genius to work in. But in one
subject our writers have led the way and are still
pre-eminent: Thoreau was the creator of a new
manner of writing about Nature. In its deeper
essence his work is inimitable, as it is the voice
of a unique personality; but in its superficial
aspects it has been taken up by a host of living
writers, who have caught something of his
method, even if they lack his genius and single-
ness of heart. From these it was an easy transition to compare Thoreau's attitude of mind with
that of Wordsworth and the other great poets of
his century who went to Nature for their inspiration, and made Nature-writing the characteristic
note of modern verse. What is it in Thoreau

that is not to be found in Byron and Shelley and
Wordsworth, not to mention old Izaak Walton,
Gilbert White of Selborne, and a host of others?
It was a rare treat, as I lay in that leafy covert,
to go over in memory the famous descriptive passages from these authors, and to contrast their
spirit with that of the book in my hand.

As I considered these matters, it seemed to me
that Thoreau's work was distinguished from that
of his American predecessors and imitators by just
these qualities of awe and wonder which we, in
our communings with Nature, so often cast away.
Mere description, though it may at times have a
scientific value, is after all a very cheap form of
literature; and, as I have already intimated, too
much curiosity of detail is likely to exert a dead-
ening influence on the philosophic and poetic contemplation of Nature. Such an influence is, as I
believe, specially noticeable at the present time,
and even Thoreau was not entirely free from its
baneful effect. Much of his writing, perhaps the
greater part, is the mere record of observation
and classification, and has not the slightest claim
on our remembrance,—unless, indeed, it possesses
some scientific value, which I doubt. Certainly
the parts of his work having permanent interest
are just those chapters where he is less the minute
observer, and more the contemplative philosopher.
Despite the width and exactness of his informa-
tion, he was far from having the truly scientific
spirit; the acquisition of knowledge, with him,

was in the end quite subordinate to his interest in
the moral significance of Nature, and the words
he read in her obscure scroll were a language of
strange mysteries, oftentimes of awe. It is a constant reproach to the prying, self-satisfied habits
of small minds to see the reverence of this great-
hearted observer before the supreme goddess he
so loved and studied.

Much of this contemplative spirit of Thoreau is
due to the soul of the man himself, to that personal force which no analysis of character can explain. But, besides this, it has always seemed to
me that, more than in any other descriptive writer
of the land, his mind is the natural outgrowth,
and his essays the natural expression, of a feeling
deep-rooted in the historical beginnings of New
England; and this foundation in the past gives a
strength and convincing force to his words that
lesser writers utterly lack. Consider the new life
of the Puritan colonists in the strange surroundings of their desert home. Consider the case of
the adventurous Pilgrims sailing from the com-
fortable city of Leyden to the unknown wilderness
over the sea. As Governor Bradford wrote, " the
place they had thoughts on was some of those
vast & unpeopled countries of America, which are
frutfull & fitt for habitation, being devoyd of all
civill inhabitants, wher ther are only salvage and
brutish men, which range up and downe, little
otherwise than ye wild beasts of the same." In
these vast and unpeopled countries, where beast

and bird were strange to the eye, and where
"salvage" men abounded,—men who did not
always make the land so "fitt" for new inhabitants as Bradford might have desired,—it was inevitable that the mind should be turned to explore
and report on natural phenomena and on savage
life.   It is a fact that some of the descriptions of
sea and land made by wanderers to Virginia and
Massachusetts have a directness and graphic
power, touched occasionally with an element of
wildness, that render them even to-day agreeable
reading.

This was before the time of Rousseau, and
before Gray had discovered the beauty of wild
mountain scenery; inevitably the early American
writers were chiefly interested in Nature as the
home of future colonists, and their books are for
the most part semi-scientific accounts of what
they studied from a utilitarian point of view.   But
the dryness of detailed description in the New
World was from the first modified and lighted up
by the wondering awe of men set down in the
midst of the strange and often threatening forces
of an untried wilderness; and this sense of awful
aloofness, which to a certain extent lay dormant
in the earlier writers, did nevertheless sink deep
into the heart of New England, and when, in the
lapse of time, the country entered into its intellectual renaissance, and the genius came who was
destined to give full expression to the thoughts
of his people before the face of Nature, it was in-

evitable that his works should be dominated by just this sense of poetic mystery.

It is this New World inheritance, moreover,—joined, of course, with his own inexplicable personality, which must not be left out of account,—that makes Thoreau's attitude toward Nature something quite distinct from that of the great poets who just preceded him. There was in him none of the fiery spirit of the revolution which caused Byron to mingle hatred of men with enthusiasm for the Alpine solitudes. There was none of the passion for beauty and the voluptuous self-abandonment of Keats; these were not in the atmosphere he breathed at Concord. He was not touched with Shelley's unearthly mysticism, nor had he ever fed

> on the aërial kisses
> Of shapes that haunt thought's wildernesses;

his moral sinews were too stark and strong for that form of mental dissipation. Least of all did he, after the manner of Wordsworth, hear in the voice of Nature any compassionate plea for the weakness and sorrow of the downtrodden. Philanthropy and humanitarian sympathies were to him a desolation and a woe. "Philanthropy is almost the only virtue which is sufficiently appreciated by mankind. Nay, it is greatly overrated; and it is our selfishness which overrates it," he writes. And again: "The philanthropist too often surrounds mankind with the remembrance of his own cast-off griefs as an atmosphere, and calls it sympathy." Similarly his reliance on the human will was too sturdy to be much perturbed by the inequalities and sufferings of mankind, and his faith in the individual was too unshaken to be led into humanitarian interest in the masses. "Alas! this is the crying sin of the age," he declares, "this want of faith in the prevalence of a man."

But the deepest and most essential difference is the lack of pantheistic reverie in Thoreau. It is this brooding over the universal spirit embodied in the material world which almost always marks the return of sympathy with Nature, and which is particularly noticeable in the writers of the past century. So Lord Byron, wracked and broken by his social catastrophes, turns for relief to the fair scenes of Lake Leman, and finds in the high mountains and placid waters a consoling spirit akin to his own.

> Are not the mountains, waves, and skies, a part
> Of me and of my soul, as I of them?

he asks; and in the bitterness of his human disappointment he would "be alone, and love Earth only for its earthly sake." Shelley, too, "mixed awful talk" with the "great parent," and heard in her voice an answer to all his vague dreams of the soul of universal love. No one, so far as I know, has yet studied the relation between Wordsworth's pantheism and his humanitarian sym-

pathies, but we need only glance at his lines on
Tintern Abbey to see how closely the two feelings
were interknit in his mind. It was because he
felt this

> sense sublime
> Of something far more deeply interfused,
> Whose dwelling is the light of setting suns,
> And the round ocean, and the living air,
> And the blue sky, and in the mind of man ;

it was because the distinctions of the human will
and the consequent perception of individual re-
sponsibility were largely absorbed in this dream of
the universal spirit, that he heard in Nature " the
still, sad music of humanity,'' and reproduced it
so sympathetically in his own song. Of all this
pantheism, whether attended with revolt from re-
sponsibility or languid reverie or humanitarian
dreams, there is hardly a trace in Thoreau. The
memory of man's struggle with the primeval
woods and fields was not so lost in antiquity that
the world had grown into an indistinguishable part
of human life. If Nature smiled upon Thoreau at
times, she was still an alien creature who succumbed only to his force and tenderness, as she had
before given her bounty, though reluctantly, to
the Pilgrim Fathers. A certain companionship
he had with the plants and wild beasts of the
field, a certain intimacy with the dumb earth; but
he did not seek to merge his personality in their
impersonal life, or look to them for a response to

2

his own inner moods; he associated with them as
the soul associates with the body.

More characteristic is his sense of awe, even of
dread, toward the great unsubdued forces of the
world. The loneliness of the mountains such as
they appeared to the early adventurers in a
strange, unexplored country; the repellent loneliness of the barren heights frowning down in-
hospitably upon the pioneer who scratched the
soil at their base; the loneliness and terror of the
dark, untrodden forests, where the wanderer
might stray away and be lost forever, where
savage men were more feared than the wild animals, and where superstition saw the haunt of
the Black Man and of all uncleanness,—all this
tradition of sombre solitude made Nature to
Thoreau something very different from the hills
and valleys of Old England. " We have not seen
pure Nature," he says, " unless we have seen her
thus vast and drear and inhuman. .   .   . Man
was not to be associated with it. It was matter,
vast, terrific,—not his Mother Earth that we have
heard of, not for him to tread on, or be buried in,
—no, it were being too familiar even to let his
bones lie there,—the home, this, of Necessity and
Fate." After reading Byron's invocation to the
Alps as the palaces of Nature; or the ethereal
mountain scenes in Shelley's *Alastor*, where all
the sternness of the everlasting hills is dissolved
into rainbow hues of shifting light as dainty as
the poet's own soul; or Wordsworth's familiar

musings in the vale of Grasmere,—if, after these,
we turn to Thoreau's account of the ascent of
Mount Katahdin, we seem at once to be in the
home of another tradition. I am tempted to
quote a few sentences of that account to emphasise the point. On the mountain heights, he says
of the beholder:

He is more lone than you can imagine. There is less
of substantial thought and fair understanding in him
than in the plains where men inhabit. His reason is dis-
persed and shadowy, more thin and subtile, like the air.
Vast, Titanic, inhuman Nature has got him at disadvan-
tage, caught him alone, and pilfers him of some of his
divine faculty. She does not smile on him as in the
plains. She seems to say sternly, Why came ye here
before your time? This ground is not prepared for you.
Is it not enough that I smile in the valleys? I have
never made this soil for thy feet, this air for thy breath-
ing, these rocks for thy neighbours. I cannot pity nor
fondle thee here, but forever relentlessly drive thee hence
to where I *am* kind.

I do not mean to present the work of Thoreau
as equal in value to the achievement of the great
poets with whom I have compared him, but wish
merely in this way to bring out more definitely
his characteristic traits. Yet if his creative genius
is less than theirs, I cannot but think his attitude
toward Nature is in many respects truer and more
wholesome. Pantheism, whether on the banks
of the Ganges or of the Thames, seems to bring
with it a spreading taint of effeminacy; and from
this the mental attitude of our Concord naturalist

was eminently free. There is something tonic
and bracing in his intercourse with the rude forces
of the forest; he went to Walden Pond because he
had "private business to transact," not for relax-
ation and mystical reverie. "To be a philosopher," he said, "is not merely to have subtle
thoughts, nor even to found a school, but so to
love wisdom as to live according to its dictates, a
life of simplicity, independence, magnanimity, and
trust;" and by recurring to the solitudes of Nature
he thought he could best develop in himself just
these manly virtues. Nature was to him a discipline of the will as much as a stimulant to the
imagination. He would, if it were possible,
"combine the hardiness of the savages with the
intellectualness of the civilised man;" and in this
method of working out the philosophical life we
see again the influence of long and deep-rooted
tradition. To the first settlers, the red man was
as much an object of curiosity and demanded as
much study as the earth they came to cultivate;
their books are full of graphic pictures of savage
life, and it should seem as if now in Thoreau this
inherited interest had received at last its ripest expression. When he travelled in the wilderness
of Maine, he was as much absorbed in learning
the habits of his Indian guides as in exploring the
woods. He had some innate sympathy or perception which taught him to find relics of old Indian
life where others would pass them by, and there
is a well-known story of his answer to one who

asked him where such relics could be discovered: he merely stooped down and picked an arrowhead from the ground.

And withal his stoic virtues never dulled his sense of awe, and his long years of observation never lessened his feeling of strangeness in the presence of solitary Nature. If at times his writing descends into the cataloguing style of the ordinary naturalist, yet the old tradition of wonder was too strong in him to be more than temporarily obscured. Unfortunately, his occasional faults have become in some of his recent imitators the staple of their talent; but Thoreau was pre-eminently the poet and philosopher of his school, and I cannot do better than close these desultory notes with the quotation of a passage which seems to me to convey most vividly his sensitiveness to the solemn mystery of the deep forest :

We heard [he writes in his *Chesuncook*], come faintly echoing, or creeping from afar, through the moss-clad aisles, a dull, dry, rushing sound, with a solid core to it, yet as if half smothered under the grasp of the luxuriant and fungus-like forest, like the shutting of a door in some distant entry of the damp and shaggy wilderness. If we had not been there, no mortal had heard it. When we asked Joe [the Indian guide] in a whisper what it was, he answered,—"Tree fall."

THE SOLITUDE OF NATHANIEL
HAWTHORNE

IN a notable passage, Hawthorne has said of his own *Twice-Told Tales* that "they have the pale tint of flowers that blossomed in too retired a shade. . . . Instead of passion there is sentiment. . . . Whether from lack of power or an unconquerable reserve, the author's touches have often an effect of tameness; the merriest man can hardly contrive to laugh at his broadest humour; the tenderest woman, one would suppose, will hardly shed warm tears at his deepest pathos." And a little further on he adds, "The sketches are not, it is hardly necessary to say, profound." Rarely has a writer shown greater skill in self-criticism than Hawthorne, except where modesty caused him to lower the truth, and in ascribing this lack of passion to his works he has struck what will seem to many the keynote of their character. When he says, however, that they are wanting in depth, he certainly errs through modesty. Many authors, great and small, display a lack of passion, but perhaps no other in all the hierarchy of poets who deal with moral problems has treated these problems, on one side at least, so profoundly as our New England romancer; and it is just this peculiarity of Hawthorne, so apparently paradoxical, which gives him his unique place among writers.

Consider for a moment *The Scarlet Letter:* the pathos of the subject, and the tragic scenes portrayed. All the world agrees that here is a masterpiece of mortal error and remorse; we are lost in admiration of the author's insight into the suffering human heart; yet has any one ever shed a tear over that inimitable romance? I think not. The book does not move us to tears; it awakens no sense of shuddering awe such as follows the perusal of the great tragedies of literature; it is not emotional, in the ordinary acceptance of the word, yet shallow or cold it certainly is not.

In the *English Note-Books* Hawthorne makes this interesting comparison of himself with Thackeray :

Mr. S—— is a friend of Thackeray [he writes], and, speaking of the last number of *The Newcomes,*—so touching that nobody can read it aloud without breaking down,—he mentioned that Thackeray himself had read it to James Russell Lowell and William Story in a cider cellar ! . . . I cannot but wonder at his coolness in respect to his own pathos, and compare it with my emotions when I read the last scene of *The Scarlet Letter* to my wife, just after writing it,—tried to read it, rather, for my voice swelled and heaved, as if I were tossed up and down on an ocean as it subsides after a storm.

Why, then, we ask, should we have tears ready for *The Newcomes*, and none for *The Scarlet*

Letter, although the pathos of the latter tale can so stir the depths of our nature as it did the author's? What curious trait in his writing, what strange attitude of the man toward the moral struggles and agony of human nature, is this that sets him apart from other novelists? I purpose to show how this is due to one dominant motive running through all his tales,—a thought to a certain extent peculiar to himself, and so persistent in its repetition that, to one who reads Hawthorne carefully, his works seem to fall together like the movements of a great symphony built upon one imposing theme.

I remember, some time ago, when walking among the Alps, that I happened on a Sunday morning to stray into the little English church at Interlaken. The room was pretty well filled with a chance audience, most of whom no doubt were, like myself, refugees from civilisation for the sake of pleasure or rest or health. The minister was a young sandy-haired Scotsman, with nothing notable in his aspect save a certain unusual look of earnestness about the eyes; and I wonder how many of my fellow listeners still remember that quiet Sabbath morn, and the sunlight streaming over all, as white and pure as if poured down from the snowy peak of the Jungfrau; and how many of them still at times see that plain little church, and the simple man standing at the pulpit, and hear the tones of his vibrating voice. Opening the Bible he paused a moment, and then read, in accents that faltered a little as if with emotion, the words, " Eloi, Eloi, lama sabachthani ?" and then paused again without adding the translation. I do not know what induced him to choose such a text, and to preach such a sermon before an audience of summer idlers; it even seemed to me that a look of surprise and perturbation stole over their faces as, in tones tremulous from the start with restrained passion, he poured forth his singular discourse. I cannot repeat his words. He told of the inevitable loneliness that follows man from the cradle to the grave; he spoke of the loneliness that lends the depth of yearning to a mother's eyes as she bends over her newborn child, for the soul of the infant has been rent from her own, and she can never again be united to what she cherished. It is this sense of individual loneliness and isolation, he said, that gives pathos to lovers' eyes when love has brought them closest together; it is this that lends austerity to the patriot's look when saluted by the acclaiming multitude. And you, he cried, who for a little while have come forth from the world into these solitudes of God, what hope ye to find ? Some respite, no doubt, from the anxiety that oppressed you in the busy town, in the midst of your loved ones about the hearth, in the crowded market place; for you believe that these solitudes of nature will speak to your hearts and comfort you, and that in the peace of nature you will find the true communion of soul that the busy world

could not give you. Yet are you deceived; for
the sympathy and power of communion between
you and this fair creation have been ruined and
utterly cast away by sin; and this was typified in
the beginning by the banishing of Adam from the
terrestrial paradise. No, the murmur of these
pleasant brooks and the whispering of these happy
leaves shall not speak to the deafened ear of your
soul; nor shall the verdure of these sunny fields
and the glory of these snowy peaks appeal to the
darkened eye of your soul: and this you shall
learn to your utter sorrow. Go back to your
homes, to your toil, to the populous deserts where
your duty lies. Go back and bear bravely the
solitude that God hath given you to bear; for this,
I declare unto you, is the burden and the penalty
laid upon us by the eternal decrees for the sin we
have done, and for the sin of our fathers before
us. Think not, while evil abides in you, ye shall
be aught but alone; for evil is the seeking of self
and the turning away from the commonalty of the
world. Your life shall indeed be solitary until
death, the great solitude, absorbs it at last. Go
back and learn righteousness and meekness; and
it may be, when the end cometh, you shall attain
unto communion with him who alone can speak
to the recluse that dwells within your breast.
And he shall comfort you for the evil of this solitude you bear; for he himself hath borne it, and
his last cry was the cry of desolation, of one forsaken and made lonely by his God.

I hope I may be pardoned for introducing memories of so personal a nature into an article of literary criticism, but there seemed no better way of indicating the predominant trait of Hawthorne's work. Other poets of the past have excelled him in giving expression to certain problems of our inner life, and in stirring the depths of our emotional nature; but not in the tragedies of Greece, or the epics of Italy, or the drama of Shakespeare will you find any presentation of this one truth of the penalty of solitude laid upon the human soul so fully and profoundly worked out as in the romances of Hawthorne. It would be tedious to take up each of his novels and tales and show how this theme runs like a sombre thread through them all, yet it may be worth while to touch on a few prominent examples.

Shortly after leaving college, Hawthorne published a novel which his maturer taste, with propriety, condemned. Despite the felicity of style which seems to have come to Hawthorne by natural right, *Fanshawe* is but a crude and conventional story. Yet the book is interesting if only to show how at the very outset the author struck the keynote of his life's work. The hero of the tale is the conventional student that figures in romance, wasted by study, and isolated from mankind by his intellectual ideals. " He had seemed, to others and to himself, a solitary being, upon whom the hopes and fears of ordinary men were ineffectual." The whole conception of the

story is a commonplace, yet a commonplace relieved by a peculiar quality in the language which
even in this early attempt predicts the stronger
treatment of his chosen theme when the artist
shall have mastered his craft.   There is, too,
something memorable in the parting scene between the hero and heroine, where Fanshawe,
having earned Ellen's love, deliberately surrenders her to one more closely associated with the
world, and himself goes back to his studies and
his death.

From this youthful essay let us turn at once to
his latest work—the novel begun when the shadow
of coming dissolution had already fallen upon him,
though still not old in years; to that " tale of the
deathless man " interrupted by the intrusion of
Death, as if in mockery of the artist's theme—

> Ah, who shall lift that wand of magic power,
>   And the lost clue regain !
> The unfinished window in Aladdin's tower
>   Unfinished must remain !

In the fragment of *The Dolliver Romance* we have,
wrought out with all the charm of Hawthorne's
maturest style, a picture of isolation caused, not
by the exclusive ambitions of youth, but by old
age and the frailty of human nature.   No extract
or comment can convey the effect of these chapters
of minute analysis, with their portrait of the old
apothecary dwelling in the time-eaten mansion,
whose windows look down on the graves of child-

ren and grandchildren he had outlived and laid
to rest.   With his usual sense of artistic contrast,
Hawthorne sets a picture of golden-haired youth
by the side of withered eld:

The Doctor's only child, poor Bessie's offspring, had
died the better part of a hundred years before, and his
grandchildren, a numerous and dimly remembered
brood, had vanished along his weary track in their
youth, maturity, or incipient age, till, hardly knowing
how it had all happened, he found himself tottering on-
ward with an infant's small fingers in his nerveless
grasp.

Again, in describing the loneliness that separates
old age from the busy current of life, Hawthorne
has recourse to a picture which he employed a
number of times, and which seems to have been
drawn from his own experience and to have
haunted his dreams.   It is the picture of a bewildered man walking the populous streets, and
feeling utterly lost and estranged in the crowd.
So the old doctor " felt a dreary impulse to elude
the people's observation, as if with a sense that he
had gone irrevocably out of fashion; . . . or
else it was that nightmare feeling which we sometimes have in dreams, when we seem to find ourselves wandering through a crowded avenue, with
the noonday sun upon us, in some wild extravagance of dress or nudity."   We are reminded by
the words of Hawthorne's own habit, during his
early Salem years, of choosing to walk abroad at
night when no one could observe him, and of his

trick in later life of hiding in the Concord woods
rather than face a passer-by on the road.

Between *Fanshawe*, with its story of the seclusion caused by youthful ambition, and *The Dolliver Romance*, with its picture of isolated old age,
there may be found in the author's successive
works every form of solitude incident to human
existence. I believe no single tale, however short
or insignificant, can be named in which, under
one guise or another, this recurrent idea does not
appear. It is as if the poet's heart were burdened
with an emotion that unconsciously dominated
every faculty of his mind; he walked through life
like a man possessed. Often while reading his
novels I have of a sudden found myself back in
the little chapel at Interlaken, listening to that
strange discourse on the penalty of sin; and the
cry of the text once more goes surging through
my ears, "Why hast thou forsaken me?" Truly
a curse is upon us; our life is rounded with im-
passable emptiness; the stress of youth, the
feebleness of age, all the passions and desires of
manhood, lead but to this inevitable solitude and
isolation of spirit.

Perhaps the first work to awaken any considerable interest in Hawthorne was the story—nôt one
of his best—of *The Gentle Boy*. The pathos of
the poor child severed by religious fanaticism
from the fellowship of the world stirred a sympathetic chord in the New England heart: and it
may even be that tears were shed over the home-

less lad clinging to his father's grave; for his
" father was of the people whom all men hate."

But far more characteristic in its weird intensity
and philosophic symbolism is the story of *The
Minister's Black Veil*. No one who has read
them has ever forgotten the dying man's fateful
words:

Why do you tremble at me alone? Tremble also at
each other! Have men avoided me, and women shown
no pity, and children screamed and fled, only for my
black veil? What, but the mystery which it obscurely
typifies, has made this piece of crape so awful? When
the friend shows his inmost heart to his friend, the lover
to his best beloved ; when man does not vainly shrink
from the eye of his Creator, loathsomely treasuring up
the secret of his sin ; then deem me a monster, for the
symbol beneath which I have lived, and die! I look
around me, and, lo! on every visage a Black Veil!

In another of the *Twice-Told Tales* the same
thought is presented in a form as ghastly as anything to be found in the pages of Poe or Hoffman.
The Lady Eleanore has come to these shores in
the early colonial days, bringing with her a heart
filled with aristocratic pride. She has, moreover,
all the arrogance of queenly beauty, and her first
entrance into the governor's mansion is over the
prostrate body of a despised lover. Her insolence
is symbolised throughout by a mantle which she
wears, of strange and fascinating splendour, embroidered for her by the fingers of a dying woman,
—a woman dying, it proves, of the smallpox, so

that the infested robe becomes the cause of a pestilence that sweeps the province. It happens now and then that Hawthorne falls into a revolting realism, and the last scene, where Lady Eleanore, perishing of the disease that has flowed from her own arrogance, is confronted by her old lover, produces a feeling in the reader almost of loathing. Yet the lady's last words are significant enough to be quoted: " The curse of Heaven hath stricken me, because I would not call man my brother, nor woman sister. I wrapped myself in PRIDE as in a MANTLE, and scorned the sympathies of nature; and therefore has nature made this wretched body the medium of a dreadful sympathy." Alas for the poor, broken creature of pride! She but suffered for electing freely a loneliness which, in one form or another, whether voluntary or involuntary, haunts all the chief persons of her creator's world. It is, indeed, characteristic of this solitude of spirit that it presents itself now as the original sin awakening Heaven's wrath, and again as itself the penalty imposed upon the guilty soul: which is but Hawthorne's way of portraying evil and its retribution as simultaneous,—nay, as one and the same thing.

But we linger too long on these minor works of our author. Much has been written about *The Scarlet Letter*, and it has been often studied as an essay in the effects of crime on the human heart. In truth, one cannot easily find, outside of Æschylus, words of brooding so profound and

single-hearted on this solemn subject; their meaning, too, should seem to be written large, yet I am
not aware that the real originality and issue of the
book have hitherto been clearly discussed. Other
poets have laid bare the workings of a diseased
conscience, the perturbations of a soul that has
gone astray; others have shown the confusion
and horror wrought by crime in the family or the
state, and something of these, too, may be found
in the effects of Dimmesdale's sin in the provincial
community; but the true moral of the tale lies in
another direction. It is a story of intertangled
love and hatred working out in four human beings the same primal curse,—love and hatred so
woven together that in the end the author asks
whether the two passions be not, after all, the
same, since each renders one individual dependent
upon another for his spiritual food, and each is in
a way an attempt to break through the boundary
that separates soul from soul. From the opening
scene at the prison door, which, "like all that
pertains to crime, seemed never to have known a
youthful era," to the final scene on the scaffold,
where the tragic imagination of the author speaks
with a power barely surpassed in the books of the
world, the whole plot of the romance moves about
this one conception of our human isolation as the
penalty of transgression.

Upon Arthur Dimmesdale the punishment falls
most painfully. From the cold and lonely heights
of his spiritual life he has stepped down, in a vain

3

endeavour against God's law, to seek the warmth of companionship in illicit love. He sins, and the very purity and fineness of his nature make the act of confession before the world almost an impossibility. The result is a strange contradiction of effects that only Hawthorne could have reconciled. By his sin Dimmesdale is more than ever cut off from communion with the world, and is driven to an asceticism and aloofness so complete that it becomes difficult for him to look any man in the eye; on the other hand, the brooding secret of his passion gives him new and powerful sympathies with life's burden of sorrow, and fills his sermons with a wonderful eloquence to stir the hearts of men. This, too, is the paradox running like a double thread through all the author's works. Out of our isolation grow the passions which but illuminate and render more visible the void from which they sprang; while, on the other hand, he is impressed by that truth which led him to say: " We are but shadows, and all that seems most real about us is but the thinnest substance of a dream,—till the heart be touched. That touch creates us,—then we begin to be,—thereby we are beings of reality and inheritors of eternity."

Opposed to the erring minister stands Roger Chillingworth, upon whom the curse acts more hideously, if not more painfully. The incommunicative student, misshapen from his birth hour, who has buried his life in books and starved his emotions to feed his brain, would draw the fair

maiden Hester into his heart, to warm that innermost chamber left lonely and chill and without a
household fire.   Out of this false and illicit desire
springs all the tragedy of the tale.   Dimmesdale
suffers for his love; but the desire of Chillingworth, because it is base, and because his character is essentially selfish, is changed into rancorous
hatred.   And here again the effect of the man's
passion is twofold: it endows him with a malig-
nant sympathy toward the object of his hate,
enabling him to play on the victim's heart as a
musician gropes among the strings of an instrument, and at the same time it severs him more
absolutely from the common weal, blotting out his
life, "as completely as if he indeed lay at the
bottom of the ocean."

   And what shall we say of the fair and piteous
Hester Prynne ?   Upon her the author has lavished
all his art: he has evoked a figure of womanhood
whose memory haunts the mind like that of another Helen.   Like Helen's, her passive beauty
has been the cause of strange trials and perturbations of which she must herself partake; she is
more human than Beatrice, nobler and larger
than Marguerite,—a creation altogether fair and
wonderful.   Yet she too must be caught in this
embroilment of evil and retribution.   The Scarlet
Letter upon her breast is compared by the author
to the brand on the brow of Cain,—a mark that
symbolises her utter separation from the mutual
joys and sorrows of the world.   She walks about

the provincial streets like some lonely bearer of a
monstrous fate. Yet because her guilt lies open
to the eyes of mankind, and because she accepts
the law of our nature, striving to aid and uplift
the faltering hearts about her without seeking re-
lease from the curse in closer human attachments,
following unconsciously the doctrine of the ancient
Hindu book,—

Therefore apply thyself unto work as thy duty bids, yet
     without attachment;
Even for the profiting of the people apply thyself unto
     work,—

because she renounces herself and the cravings of
self, we see her gradually glorified in our presence,
until the blessings of all the poor and afflicted follow her goings about, and the Scarlet Letter, ceasing to be a stigma of scorn, becomes " a type of
something to be sorrowed over, and looked upon
with awe, yet with reverence too."

As a visible outcome of the guilty passion little
Pearl stands before us, an elfin child that " lacked
reference and adaptation to the world into which
she was born," and that lived with her mother in
a " circle of seclusion from human society."   But
the suffering of the parents is efficient finally to
set their child free from the curse; and at the last,
when the stricken father proclaims his guilt in
public and acknowledges his violation of the law,
we see Pearl kissing him and weeping, and her
tears are a pledge that she is to grow up amid

common joys and griefs, nor forever do battle with the world.

And in the end what of the love between Arthur and Hester? Was it redeemed of shame, and made prophetic of a perfect union beyond the grave? Alas, there is something pitiless and awful in the last words of the two, as the man lies on the scaffold, dying in her arms:

"Shall we not meet again?" whispered she, bending her face down close to his. "Shall we not spend our immortal life together? Surely, surely, we have ransomed one another, with all this woe! Thou lookest far into eternity, with those bright dying eyes! Then tell me what thou seest?"

"Hush, Hester, hush!" said he, with tremulous solemnity. "The law we broke!—the sin here so awfully revealed!—let these alone be in thy thoughts! I fear! I fear! It may be that, when we forgot our God,—when we violated our reverence each for the other's soul,—it was thenceforth vain to hope that we could meet hereafter, in an everlasting and pure reunion."

With his next novel Hawthorne enters upon a new phase of his art. Henceforth he seems to have brooded not so much on the immediate effect of evil as on its influence when handed down in a family from generation to generation, and symbolised (for his mind must inevitably speak through symbols) by the ancestral fatality of gurgling blood in the throat or by the print of a bloody footstep. But whatever the symbol employed, the

moral outcome of the ancient wrong is always the
same: in *Septimius Felton*, in *The Dolliver Romance*, and most of all in *The House of the Seven
Gables*, the infection of evil works itself out in the
loneliness of the last sufferers, and their isolation
from the world.

It is not my intention to analyse in detail Hawthorne's remaining novels. As for *The House of
the Seven Gables*, we know what unwearied care
the author bestowed on the description of Miss
Hepzibah Pyncheon, alone in the desolate family
mansion, and on her grotesque terrors when forced
to creep from her seclusion; and how finely he has
painted the dim twilight of alienation from himself and from the world into which the wretched
Clifford was thrust! And Judge Pyncheon, the
portly, thick-necked, scheming man of action,—
who, in imagination, does not perceive him, at
last, sitting in the great oaken chair, fallen asleep
with wide-staring eyes while the watch ticks
noisily in his hand? Asleep, but none shall
arouse him from that slumber, and warn him that
the hour of his many appointments is slipping by.
What immutable mask of indifference has fallen
upon his face? " The features are all gone: there
is only the paleness of them left. And how looks
it now? There is no window! There is no face!
An infinite, inscrutable blackness has annihilated
sight! Where is our universe? All crumbled
away from us; and we, adrift in chaos, may
hearken to the gusts of homeless wind, that go

sighing and murmuring about, in quest of what was once a world! Is there no other sound? One other, and a fearful one. It is the ticking of the Judge's watch, which, ever since Hepzibah left the room in search of Clifford, he has been holding in his hand. Be the cause what it may, this little, quiet, never ceasing throb of Time's pulse, repeating its small strokes with such busy regularity, in Judge Pyncheon's motionless hand, has an effect of terror, which we do not find in any other accompaniment of the scene.''

Many times, while reading this story and the others that involve an ancestral curse, I have been struck by something of similarity and contrast at once between our New England novelist and Æschylus, the tragic poet of Athens. It should seem at first as if the vast gap between the civilisations that surrounded the two writers and the utterly different forms of their art would preclude any real kinship; and yet I know not where, unless in these late romances, any companion can be found in modern literature to the Orestean conception of satiety begetting insolence, and insolence calling down upon a family the inherited curse of Atè. It may be reckoned the highest praise of Hawthorne that his work can suggest any such comparison with the masterpiece of Æschylus, and not be entirely emptied of value by the juxtaposition. But if Æschylus and Hawthorne are alike poets of Destiny and of the fateful inheritance of woe, their methods of portraying the power and handiwork of Atè are perfectly distinct. The Athenian too represents Orestes, the last inheritor of the curse, as cut off from the fellowship of mankind; but to recall the Orestean tale, with all its tragic action of murder and matricide and frenzy, is to see in a clearer light the originality of Hawthorne's conception of moral retribution in the disease of inner solitude. There is in the difference something, of course, of the constant distinction between classic and modern art; but added to this is the creative idealism of Hawthorne's rare and elusive genius.

I have dwelt at some length on *The Scarlet Letter* and *The House of the Seven Gables*, because they are undoubtedly the greatest of Hawthorne's romances and the most thoroughly permeated with his peculiar ideas,—works so nearly perfect, withal, in artistic execution that the mind of the reader is overwhelmed by a sense of the power and self-restraint possible to human genius.

Over the other two long novels we must pass lightly, although they are not without bearing on the subject in hand. *The Blithedale Romance*, being in every way the slightest and most colourless of the novels, would perhaps add little to the discussion. But in *The Marble Faun* it would be interesting to study the awakening of Donatello's half-animal nature to the fullness of human sympathies by his love for Miriam; and to follow Miriam herself, moving, with the dusky veil of secrecy about her, amidst the crumbling ruins and living realities of Rome like some phantom of the city's long-buried tragedies. Hawthorne never made known the nature of the shadow that hovered over this exotic creature, and it may be that he has here indulged in a piece of pure mystification; but for my own part I could never resist the conviction that she suffers for the same cause as Shelley's Beatrice Cenci. Granting such a conjecture to be well founded, it would throw light on our thesis to compare the two innocent victims of the same hideous crime: to observe the frenzy aroused in Beatrice by her wrong, and the passion of her acts, and then to look upon the silent, unearthly Miriam, snatched from the hopes of humanity, and wrapped in the shadows of impenetrable isolation. Powerful as is the story of the Cenci, to me, at least, the fate of Miriam is replete with deeper woe and more transcendent meaning.

It is natural that the reader of these strange stories and stranger confessions should ask, almost with a shudder, what manner of man was the author. We do not wonder that his family, in their printed memoirs, should have endeavoured in every way to set forth the social and sunny side of his character, and should have published the *Note-Books* with the avowed purpose of dispelling the "often-expressed opinion that Mr. Hawthorne was gloomy and morbid." Let us admit with them that he had but the " inevitable pensiveness and gravity " of one to whom has been given "the

awful power of insight." No one supposes for a
moment that Hawthorne's own mind was clouded
with the remorseful consciousness of secret guilt;
and we are ready to accept his statement that he
had " no love of secrecy and darkness," and that
his extreme reserve had only made his writings
more objective.

Morbid in any proper sense of the word Hawthorne cannot be called, except in so far as
throughout his life he cherished one dominant
idea, and that a peculiar state of mental isolation
which destroys the illusions leading to action, and
so tends at last to weaken the will; and there are,
it must be confessed, signs in the maturer age of
Hawthorne that his will actually succumbed to
the attacks of this subtle disillusionment. But
beyond this there is in his work no taint of un-
wholesomeness, unless it be in itself unwholesome
to be possessed by one absorbing thought. We
have no reason to discredit his own statement:
" When I write anything that I know or suspect
is morbid, I feel as though I had told a lie." Nor
was he even a mystery-monger: the mysterious
element in his stories, which affects some prosaic
minds as a taint of morbidness, is due to the intense symbolism of his thought, to the intrinsic
and unconscious mingling of the real and the
ideal. Like one of his own characters, he could
" never separate the idea from the symbol in
which it manifests itself." Yet the idea is always
there. He is strong both in analysis and general-

isation; there is no weakening of the intellectual faculties. Furthermore, his pages are pervaded with a subtle ironical humour hardly compatible with morbidness,—not a boisterous humour that awakens laughter, but the mood, half quizzical and half pensive, of a man who stands apart and smiles at the foibles and pretensions of the world. Now and then there is something rare and unexpected in his wit, as, for example, in his comment on the Italian mosquitoes : " They are bigger than American mosquitoes ; and if you crush them, after one of their feasts, it makes a terrific blood spot. It is a sort of suicide to kill them." And if there is to be found in his tales a fair share of disagreeable themes, yet ·he never confounds things of good and evil report, nor things fair and foul; the moral sense is intact. Above all, there is no undue appeal to the sensations or emotions.

Rather it is true, as we remarked in the beginning, that the lack of outward emotion, together with their poignancy of silent appeal, is a distinguishing mark of Hawthorne's writings. The thought underlying all his work is one to trouble the depths of our nature, and to stir in us the sombrest chords of brooding, but it does not move us to tears or passionate emotion: those affections are dependent on our social faculties, and are starved in the rarefied air of his genius. Hawthorne indeed relates that the closing chapters of *The Scarlet Letter*, when read aloud to his wife, sent her to bed with a sick headache. And yet, as a judicious critic has observed, this may have been in part just because the book seals up the fountain of tears.

It needs but a slight acquaintance with his own letters and *Note-Books*, and with the anecdotes current about him, to be assured that never lived a man to whom ordinary contact with his fellows was more impossible, and that the mysterious solitude in which his fictitious characters move is a mere shadow of his own imperial loneliness of soul. "I have made a captive of myself," he writes in a letter of condolence to Longfellow, "and put me into a dungeon, and now I cannot find the key to let myself out; and if the door were open, I should be almost afraid to come out. You tell me that you have met with troubles and changes. I know not what these may have been, but I can assure you that trouble is the next best thing to enjoyment, and that there is no fate in this world so horrible as to have no share in its joys or sorrows." Was ever a stranger letter of condolence penned?

Even the wider sympathies of the race seem to have been wanting in the man as they are wanting in his books. It is he who said of himself, "Destiny itself has often been worsted in the attempt to get me out to dinner." Though he lived in the feverish ante-bellum days, he was singularly lacking in the political sense, and could look with indifference on the slave question. When at last the war broke out, and he was forced into

sympathies foreign to his nature, it seemed as if
something gave way within him beneath the un-
accustomed stress. It is said, and with probable
truth, that the trouble of his heart actually caused
his death. His novels are full of brooding over
the past, but of real historic sympathy he had
none. He has mentioned the old Concord fight
almost with contempt, and in his travels the
homes of great men and the scenes of famous
deeds rarely touched him with enthusiasm.
Strangest of all, in a writer of such moral depth,
is his coldness toward questions of religion. So
marked was this apathy that George Ripley is re-
ported to have said on the subject of Hawthorne's
religious tendencies, " There were none, no reverence in his nature." He was not sceptical, to
judge from his occasional utterances, but simply
indifferent; the matter did not interest him. He
was by right of inheritance a Puritan; all the intensity of the Puritan nature remained in him,
and all the overwhelming sense of the heinousness
of human depravity, but these, cut off from the old
faith, took on a new form of their own. Where
the Puritan teachers had fulminated the vengeance of an outraged God, Hawthorne saw only
the infinite isolation of the errant soul. In one of
his stories, in many ways the most important of
his shorter works, he has chosen for his theme the
Unpardonable Sin, and it is interesting to read the
tale side by side with some of the denunciatory
sermons of the older divines.

It is not necessary to repeat the story of *Ethan Brand*, the lime burner, who, in the wilderness of the mountains, in the silences of the night while he fed the glowing furnace, conceived the idea of producing in himself the Unpardonable Sin. Every one must remember how at last he found his quest in his own wretched heart that had refused to beat in human sympathy, and had regarded the men about him as so many problems to be studied. In the end, he who had denied the brotherhood of man, and spurned the guidance of the stars, and who now refuses to surrender his body back to the bosom of Mother Earth,— in the end he must call on the deadly element of fire as his only friend, and so, with blasphemy on his lips, flings himself into the flaming oven. It is a sombre and weird catastrophe, but the tragic power of the scene lies in the picture of utter loneliness in the guilty breast. And would you hear by its side the denunciations of our greatest theologian against sin? Read but a paragraph from the sermons of Jonathan Edwards:

The God that holds you over the pit of hell, much as one holds a spider or some loathsome insect over the fire, abhors you, and is dreadfully provoked. . . . If you cry to God to pity you, he will be so far from pitying you in your doleful case, or showing you the least regard or favour, that, instead of that, he will only tread you underfoot. . . . And though he will know that you cannot bear the weight of omnipotence treading upon you, yet he will not regard that; but he will crush you under his feet without mercy; he will crush out your blood and make it fly, and it shall be sprinkled on his garments, so as to stain all his raiment.

Is it a wonder that strong men were moved to tears and women fainted beneath such words? Yet in the still hours of meditation there is to us, at least, something more appalling in the gloomy imaginations of Hawthorne, because they are founded more certainly on everlasting truth.

I have spoken as if the mental attitude of Hawthorne was one common to the race, however it may be exaggerated in form by his own inner vision; and to us of the western world, over whom have passed centuries of Christian brooding, and who find ourselves suddenly cut loose from the consolation of Christian faith, his voice may well seem the utterance of universal experience, and we may be even justified in assuming that his words have at last expressed what has long slumbered in human consciousness. His was not the bitterness, the fierce indignation of loneliness, that devoured the heart of Swift; nor yet the terror of a soul like Cowper's, that believed itself guilty of the unpardonable sin, and therefore condemned to everlasting exile and torment; nor Byron's personal rancour and hatred of society; nor the ecstasy of Thomas à Kempis, whose spirit was rapt away out of the turmoil of existence; but rather an intensification of the solitude that invests the modern world, and by right found its deepest expression in the New England heart.

Not with impunity had the human race for ages
dwelt on the eternal welfare of the soul; for from
such meditation the sense of personal importance
had become exacerbated to an extraordinary degree. What could result from such teaching as
that of Jonathan Edwards but an extravagant
sense of individual existence, as if the moral gov-
ernance of the world revolved about the action of
each mortal soul? And when the alluring faith
attendant on this form of introspection paled, as it
did during the so-called transcendental movement
into which Hawthorne was born, there resulted
necessarily a feeling of anguish and bereavement
more tragic than any previous moral stage through
which the world had passed. The loneliness of
the individual, which had been vaguely felt and
lamented by poets and philosophers of the past,
took on a poignancy altogether unexampled. It
needed but an artist with the vision of Hawthorne
to represent this feeling as the one tragic calamity
of mortal life, as the great primeval curse of sin.
What lay dormant in the teaching of Christianity
became the universal protest of the human heart.

In no way can we better estimate the universality, and at the same time the modern note,
of Hawthorne's solitude than by turning for a
moment to the literature of the far-off Ganges.
There, too, on the banks of the holy river, men
used much to ponder on the life of the human
soul in its restless wandering from birth to birth;
and in their books we may read of a loneliness as

profound as Hawthorne's, though quite distinct
in character.   To them, also, we are born alone,
we die alone, and alone we reap the fruits of our
good and evil deeds.   The dearest ties of our
earthly existence are as meaningless and transient
as the meeting of spar with drifting spar on the
ocean waves.   Yet in all this it is the isolation of the
soul from the source of universal life that troubles
human thought; there is no cry of personal anguish here, such as arises from Christianity, for
the loss of individuality is ever craved by the
Hindu as the highest good.   And besides this
distinction between the Western and Eastern
forms of what may be called secular solitude, the
Hindu carried the idea into abstract realms
whither no Occidental can penetrate.

> HE, in that solitude before
> The world was, looked the wide void o'er
> And nothing saw, and said, Lo, I
> Alone!—and still we echo the lone cry.
>
> Thereat He feared, and still we fear
> In solitude when naught is near:
> And, Lo, He said, myself alone!
> What cause of dread when second is not known!

But into this dim region of Oriental mysticism
we have no reason to intrude.   We may at least
count it among the honours of our literature that
it was left for a denizen of this far Western land,
living in the midst of a late-born and confused
civilisation, to give artistic form to a thought that,

4

in fluctuating form, has troubled the minds of philosophers from the beginning. Other authors may be greater in so far as they touch our passions more profoundly, but to the solitude of Nathaniel Hawthorne we owe the most perfect utterance of a feeling that must seem to us now as old and as deep as life itself.

It would be easy to explain Hawthorne's peculiar temperament, after the modern fashion, by reference to heredity and environment. No doubt there was a strain of eccentricity in the family. He himself tells of a cousin who made a spittoon out of the skull of his enemy; and it is natural that a descendant of the old Puritan witch judge should portray the weird and grotesque aspects of life. Probably this native tendency was increased by the circumstances that surrounded his youth: the seclusion of his mother's life ; his boyhood on Lake Sebago, where, as he says, he first got his "cursed habit of solitude;" and the long years during which he lived as a hermit in Salem. But, after all, these external matters, and even the effect of heredity so far as we can fathom it, explain little or nothing. A thousand other men might have written his books if their source lay in such antecedents. Behind it all was the dæmonic force of the man himself, the everlasting mystery of genius habiting in his brain, and choosing him to be an exemplar and interpreter of the inviolable individuality in which lie the pain and glory of our human estate.

THE ORIGINS OF HAWTHORNE AND POE

WE are credibly told that in years not so very long past young women and even grave men used to read the Gothic tales of Ann Radcliffe with tense brows and trembling lips; and the essays of Carlyle still stand a voluble witness to prove how seriously the grotesque marvels of German romance were once accepted in England. Mrs. Radcliffe is no doubt read occasionally to-day, and the indefatigable Mr. Lang has even attempted to reinstate her in popular favour. But her most generous admirer could hardly aver that she was anything more to him than a curious amusement; the horror of her tales has vanished away like the moonlight she was so fond of describing. And as for Tieck and Wackenroder and all that dim romantic crew of Teuton *Sturm* and *Drang*—not even an Andrew Lang has arisen for them.

It is a matter for reflection, therefore, that in this country a new life of Hawthorne [1] should be

[1] *Nathaniel Hawthorne.* By George E. Woodberry. [American Men of Letters.] Boston: Houghton Mifflin & Co.

something of a literary event and that there should
be a sufficient public to warrant the issue of two
new and elaborate editions of Poe;[1] for at first
thought it might seem that both Hawthorne and
Poe fall in the same class with those forgotten
weavers of moonlight and mysticism.   What is it,
indeed, that gives vitality to their work and separates it from the ephemeral product of English
and German Gothicism?   More than that: Why
is it that the only two writers of America who
have won almost universal renown as artists are
these romancers, each of whom is, after his own
manner, a sovereign in that strange region of
emotion which we name the weird?   Other work
they have done, and done well, but when we call
to mind their distinguishing productions we think
first of such scenes as *The Fall of the House of
Usher*, *The Raven*, and *The Sleeper*, or of such
characters as Arthur Dimmesdale with his morbid
remorse and unearthly sufferings, the dreamlike
existence of Clifford, the hideous unexplained
mystery of Miriam's wrong, and the awful search
of Ethan Brand — scenes and characters which
belong to the real world, for they appeal to a
sympathetic chord in our own breasts, but which
are yet quite overlaid with some insistent shadow
of the fantastic realm of symbolism.

Hawthorne ascribes the superiority of Nature's
work over man's to the fact " that the former

[1] Published respectively by Thomas Y. Crowell & Co.
and by G. P. Putnam's Sons.

works from the innermost germ, while the latter
works merely superficially,'' and the same explanation may be given of the genuineness of his
own work and Poe's in comparison with the unreality of Mrs. Radcliffe or Tieck; the weird, unearthly substance moulded by their genius is from
the innermost core of the national consciousness.
Their achievement is not like the Gothic novel
introduced into England by Horace Walpole, a
mere dilettante; there is in them very little of that
recrudescence of mediæval superstition and gloom
which marked the rise of romanticism in Europe,
little or nothing of the knights and ladies, turrets
and dungeons and all that tawdry paraphernalia,
and, fortunately for their reputation, no taint of
that peculiar form of sentimentalism which pervades the German *Herzensergiessungen* like the
odour of Schiller's decaying apples. Their work
is the last efflorescence of a tradition handed down
to them unbroken from the earliest Colonial days,
and that tradition was the voice of a stern and in-
domitable moral character. The unearthly visions
of Poe and Hawthorne are in no wise the result
of literary whim or of unbridled individualism,
but are deep-rooted in American history. Neither
Professor Woodberry in his Life of Hawthorne
nor Professor Harrison in his Life of Poe has, it
seems to me, brought out with due emphasis these
spiritual origins of a school of romance which is
so unique in its way as to have made for itself a
sure place in the literature of the world.

The name of Hawthorne carries us back at once
to those grim days of his ancestor in Salem Village
when for a season almost the whole community
gave itself up to the frenzy of witch hunting.   In
the earlier days the superstitions of England were
concerned chiefly with the fairy folk of hearth and
field, a quaint people commonly, and kindly disposed, if mischievous.   But with the advent of
Puritanism came a change; the fair and frolicsome
play of the fancy was discredited and the starved
imagination had its revenge.   In place of the
elves and goblins of a freer age, instead of "Robin
Goodfellow, the spoorn, the man-in-the-oak, the
hellwain, the firedrake, the puckle" and all that
antic crew, the imagination now evoked the terrific spectre of the Devil and attributed to his personal agency all the mishaps of life.   Hence it is
that witchcraft became so much more prominent
with the Reformation and reached its height
where Puritan feelings prevailed.   On the one
hand it was employed by the Roman Church as
an aid in its exterminating fight with the Wal-
denses and other heretics—the good monks no
doubt being easily persuaded, where persuasion
was necessary, that the ascetic revolt against the
office of the imagination in worship was of dia-
bolic origin—and, on the other hand, the Protest-
ants, and particularly the Puritans with their
morbid horror of sin, were quick to accredit to the
author of sin every phenomenon they could not
understand.   Witchcraft, to be sure, is as old as

history, and we need go no further abroad than
the classic poets for tales of the most abominable
night hags.   But there is this difference between
such monsters as Lucan's Erichtho and the abor-
tions of Christian demonology: Erichtho may
haunt the sepulchres and breathe into the cold
mouths of the dead the dark secret she would
transmit to the Shades, but in the end she is only
a product of the imagination brooding on things
unclean and hideous; there is in the dread and repugnance she inspires no such added horror as
that which the Christian felt at the thought of a
soul leagued for infamous ends with the Prince of
Hell and doomed as a rebel against God to everlasting tortures.

Considering the history of the Puritan emi-
grants we shall not be surprised to find these superstitions breaking out with peculiar virulence
in the New World.   Persecution and insult at
home had not tended to soften their temper, nor
did flight across a waste of perilous waters to a
wilderness where everything was strange and unexplored bring light and cheerfulness to their
imagination.   In England at least their morbid
intensity was to some extent modified by contact
with the worldly life about them; in their new
home they were completely given up to the working out of their stern purposes.   Terrors and difficulties only added fuel to their zeal.   "Our faithers
were Englishmen which came over this great
ocean and were ready to perish in this wilder-

ness," says old Governor Bradford; and " with
what difficulties [they] wrastled in going throug
these things," we may read in all our school-
books. It is easy to see how these hardships and
these bitterly-won victories increased the sternness
and unyieldingness of the New England Puritans,
but perhaps we do not often consider the influence
exerted on their imaginations by the wild country
and wilder "salvages," as they called the red men,
that now engaged their attention. They no longer
beheld about them the pleasant vales and green
hills of Old England, which the long habitation of
man had rendered almost human, but the vast and
pathless forests of the wilderness, where nature appeared under a new and forbidding aspect. There
is at the best something weird and uncannny
about the great woods into whose depths the eye
cannot penetrate and from whose interwoven
shadows, especially when night has fallen and the
ear has grown painfully alert, come forth at intervals sounds that seem to indicate the activity of
some nameless secret life within the darkness.
What then must have been the feelings of the
New England farmer as perchance he made his
way homeward at sundown along the border of
the gloomy forest. The kindly fancy of his an-
cestors who peopled the woods with mischievous
goblins had yielded to his belief in the extended
powers of evil. In these deep shadows he knew
not but the very enemy of God might be lurking
to lure him to destruction. It was no pleasant

waldeinsamkeit he felt, such as romantic poets love to indulge, but awe and ghostly terror.

And this feeling was exaggerated by the actual savages who inhabited the woods. The settlers were for the most part thoroughly convinced that these poor, brutal denizens of the wilderness were under the special tutelage of Satan. In times of distress the colonists were ready to charge all their calamities to the machinations of an infernal conspiracy.

It was afterward by *them* [the Indians] confessed, [says Cotton Mather in his *Magnalia*], that upon the arrival of the *English* in these parts, the *Indians* employed their *sorcerers*, whom they call *powaws*, like *Balaam*, to curse them, and let loose their *demons* upon them, to shipwreck them, to distract them, to poison them, or any way to ruin them. All the noted *powaws* in the country spent three days together in diabolical *conjurations*, to obtain the assistance of the *devils* against the settlement of these our *English*.

It is not strange, therefore, that when the delusion of witchcraft fell upon these people it should have assumed a peculiarly tragic aspect. They were dwelling in the midst of hostile demonic powers, and, feeling themselves attacked, they turned upon the enemy with all the strength and intensity of their souls. And how real and material the phenomena appeared to the bewildered onlookers may be gathered from this sulfurous account written by an eyewitness of the sufferings of one of the victims:

Margaret Rule would sometimes have her jaws forcibly pulled open, whereupon something invisible would be poured down her throat: we all saw her swallow, and yet we saw her try all she could, by spitting, coughing, and shrieking, that she might not swallow; but one time the standers-by plainly saw something of that odd liquor itself on the outside of her neck; she cried out of it, as if scalding brimstone were poured into her, and the whole house would immediately scent so hot of brimstone that we were scarce able to endure it.

Under the stress of this morbid excitement the good people of Salem and the neighbourhood were thrown into a frenzy of fear; crops were abandoned, business stood still, and the only matters considered were the horrible persecutions of Satan in their midst. The general feeling of alarm was aggravated to something like desperation when the Rev. Deodat Lawson in the meeting-house of Salem village preached an inflammatory sermon in which he charged the outburst of the infernal powers directly to the sins of the people.

You are therefore to be deeply humbled, [he said,] and sit in the dust, considering the signal hand of God in singling out this place, this poor village, for the first seat of Satan's tyranny, and to make it (as 't were) the rendezvous of devils, where they muster their infernal forces; appearing to the afflicted as coming armed to carry on their malicious designs against the bodies, and, if God in mercy prevent not, against the souls of many in this place.

No wonder that the people did actually believe " that the devils were walking about our streets with lengthened chains, making a dreadful noise in our ears; and brimstone (even without a metaphor) was making a horrid and a hellish stench in our nostrils."

To stop these terrible inroads of Satan a special court was created, before which those previously examined were tried. Those found guilty were hanged on a conspicuous eminence which thus acquired the ominous title of witch-hill; and how awful was the spectacle there presented to the panic-stricken people may be gathered from the pious ejaculation of the Reverend Mr. Noyes, "What a sad thing it is to see eight firebrands of hell hanging there!" The cruelty engendered by this feeling of insecurity is well indicated by the treatment of Giles Corey, who, refusing to plead either guilty or not guilty, was subjected to the *peine dure et forte*, as the tale is related in Longfellow's *New England Tragedy;* but Longfellow does not relate what we are told in a ballad of the period, that when from the oppression of the stone on his chest Corey's tongue protruded it was rudely thrust back by the staff of a bystander.

In due time this "hellish molestation," as one of the persecuted called it, came to a sudden end; but not before twenty victims had suffered death, many had died in jail, hundreds had endured imprisonment in its worst forms, whole families had been impoverished, and a moral impression had been made upon the community which nothing could efface. The modern historian of the delu-

sion tells us that a sort of curse still rests on the
immediate scene of these tragic events and that
neglect and desertion still brood on the accursed
spot.

Were we to go no further than this episode of
Salem history we should find it easy to explain
by inheritance that mystic brooding over the dark
and intricate effects of sin which the descendant
of old John Hathorne has made the substance of
his romance, or to account for the realism that
underlies the wild fantasies of Poe. And we need
only to dip into Cotton Mather's voluminous record of the dealings of Providence in America to
see how intensely the mind of the Puritans was
occupied with unearthly matters and what a leg-
acy of emotions approaching the weird was left by
them to posterity. When the faith of these mili-
tant saints was untroubled it often assumed a
sweetness and fullness of spiritual content that
might even pass into rapturous delight. But always this intoxicating joy bordered on the region
of awe—the awe of a soul in the presence of the
great and ineffable mysteries of holiness; and the
life of Thomas Shepard, which Mather calls "*a
trembling walk with God*," may not unfitly be
taken to illustrate the peculiar temper of their religion. And if in the wisest and sanest of the
Puritan Fathers this trembling solicitude was
never far away, there were others in whom the
fear of the Lord became a mania of terror. Consider what the impression on the minds of child-

ren must have been when in the midst of their
innocent sport the awful apparition of the Rev.
James Noyes stood before them and rebuked them
into silence with these solemn words: " Cousins,
I wonder you can be so merry, unless you are
sure of your salvation!" Consider the spiritual
state of a young man, celebrated for his godliness,
who could note down in his diary with curious
precision: "I was almost in the *suburbs of hell* all
day."

Literature, in the true sense of the word, could
not well flourish among a people who saw in the
plastic imagination a mere seduction of the senses,
and whose intellectual life was thus absorbed in
theological speculation. To be sure, a good deal
of verse was written and even printed in early
Colonial days; but of all the poets of that age only
one attained any real celebrity and has in a way
lived on into the present. Michael Wigglesworth,
the faithful pastor of Malden, where in the odour
of sanctity he died in 1705, is described as " a
little feeble *shadow* of a *man* ;" but his diminutive
frame harboured a mighty spirit. His poems
breathed the very quintessence of Puritan faith,
and as such obtained immediate and extraordinary popularity. Professor Tyler calculates that
in the first year of publication his *Day of Doom*
was purchased by at least one in every thirty-five
persons of New England; printed as a common
ballad it was hawked everywhere about the country, and its lugubrious stanzas were even taught

to children along with the catechism.   As late as
the year 1828 an essayist declared that many an
aged person of his acquaintance could still repeat
the poem, though they might not have seen a copy
of it since they were in leading strings; and
in his own time Cotton Mather had thought it
might " perhaps find our children till the day itself arrives "—which God forbid.

The strength of Master Wigglesworth's genius,
in this picture of the *Day of Doom*, is, as we
should expect, devoted to those who

> void of tears, but fill'd with fears,
>   and dreadful expectation
> Of endless pains and scalding flames,
>   stand waiting for Damnation.

One after another the various kinds of sinners are
arraigned at the bar and receive their due reward.
Most hideous and most famous of all are the
stanzas that describe the pleading and condemnation of unbaptised infants.   As an expression of
the grotesque in literature they are not without a
kind of crude power; as the voice of a real and
tremendously earnest faith they elude the grasp
of a modern mind, one can only shudder and avert
his eyes.   We contrast with some curiosity and
no little bewilderment the unflinching frankness
of this earlier Calvinist with the shifting creed
of a recent Calvinistic convention which has attempted to explain away the catechism's abandon-
ment of non-elect infants.   Yet Wigglesworth,

like the Presbyterians of to-day, had his moment
of compunction for the poor souls who

> from the womb unto the tomb
> Were straightway carriëd;—

he at least allowed to them " the easiest room in
hell!" Those simple words have of recent years
acquired a certain notoriety through literary hand
books; indeed, for naked and appalling realism of
horror, when all is considered, it would not be
easy to find a verse to surpass them.

Wigglesworth's rhymes were, as I said, the
intellectual food of the young, and some such
strong meat would seem necessary to prepare
them for the sermons that nourished their manhood. And at least one of these sermons, Jonathan Edwards's famous Enfield discourse of
Sinners in the Hands of an Angry God, has
gained the unenviable reputation of being perhaps
the most tremendous and uncompromising enunciation ever made of the gloomier side of Calvin-
ism. His picture of worldly men hanging over
the pit of hell " by a slender thread, with the
flames of divine wrath flashing about it, and
ready every moment to singe it and burn it asunder," has become classical in its own way.

After the death of Edwards, in 1758, the heart
of the country became more and more absorbed in
the impending conflict of the Revolution. For
a while, at least, religion and the terrors of damnation must give place to the more imminent peril

of political subjugation. In New England that other phase of Puritanism, the spirit that had led Cromwell and his Ironsides to victory, and had established the liberties of the English constitution, came to the foreground, and for a time the political pamphlet usurped the place of the sermon. But even then literature did not entirely vanish; and at intervals through the rasping cries of revolution one may catch a note of that pensiveness or gloom, that habitual dwelling on the supernatural significance of life, which had come to be the dominant intellectual tone of the country. Indeed, it was this violent wrenching of the national consciousness into new fields which brought about the change from the old supernaturalism of religion to the shadowy symbolism of literature as exemplified in Hawthorne and Poe. We seem to see the beginning of this new spirit in the haunting pathos that throbs through the anonymous ballad of *Nathan Hale :*

The breezes went steadily through the tall pines,
  A saying, " Oh! hu-ush! " a saying, "Oh! hu-ush! "
As stilly stole by a bold legion of horse,
  For Hale in the bush, for Hale in the bush.

" Keep still," said the thrush as she nestled her young,
    In a nest by the road; in a nest by the road;
" For the tyrants are near and with them appear
    What bodes us no good; what bodes us no good."

Of all the gentlemen—and women, too—who wrote verse in those stirring times only one can

lay claim to any genuine poetic inspiration.
Philip Freneau, of New Jersey, has even yet a
slight hold on the memory of the reading public,
and would be more read and better known were
his works subjected to proper selection and edit-
ing. Like all the other versifiers of the period
Freneau was caught in the wild vortex of political affairs, and, against the protests of his truer
nature as he himself avows, gave up the gentler
muses for the raucous voice of satire. But here
and there through his works we find a suggestion
of what he might have accomplished had he fallen
on better times. In him we catch perhaps the
first note of the weird as it appears in our later
literature, of that transition of overwhelming
superstition into shadowy haunting symbolism.
Not unseldom a stanza, or a single line it may
be, wakes an echo in the mind curiously like Poe.
Such, for instance, is the spectral beauty of that
stanza of *The Indian Burying Ground*, whose last
line, as Poe once pointed out, was borrowed intact,
and never acknowledged, by Campbell:

> By midnight moons, o'er moistening dews,
>   In vestments for the chase arrayed,
> The hunter still the deer pursues,
>   The hunter and the deer—a shade.

A glance at the titles of Freneau's poems would
show how persistently, when relieved from the
immediate pressure of politics, his mind reverted
to subjects of decay and quiet dissolution. In

5

one of his longer poems, *The House of Death*, he
has just failed of achieving a work which might
have come from the brain of Poe himself.   At
the hour of midnight the poet dreams that he
wanders over a desolate country:

> Dark was the sky, and not one friendly star
>   Shone from the zenith or horizon, clear,
> Mist sate upon the woods, and darkness rode
>   In her black chariot, with a wild career.
>
> And from the woods the late resounding note
>   Issued of the loquacious whip-poor-will,
> Hoarse, howling dogs, and nightly roving wolves
>   Clamour'd from far off cliffs invisible.

At last he finds himself in the presence of " a
noble dome raised fair and high," standing in the
midst of " a mournful garden of autumnal hue ":

> The poppy there, companion to repose,
>   Displayed her blossoms that began to fall,
> And here the purple amaranthus rose
>   With mint strong scented, for the funeral.

In this strange spot, which has something of
the unearthly qualities of Rappaccini's garden or
Poe's spectral landscapes, stands the desolate
home of a young man whose ˙beloved consort
death has recently snatched away, and who now
harbours as a guest the grisly person of Death
himself.   Death, stretched on the couch and surrounded by ghoulish phantoms, lies dying.   Over
the conversation that ensues and the blasphemies
of the ghastly sufferer we may pass without de-

laying. At last after Death has composed his own
epitaph and described the tomb he is to occupy,
in

> A burying-yard of sinners dead, unblest,

the poet flees terror-smitten out of that house
into the tempestuous night.

> Nor looked I back, till to a far off wood
>   Trembling with fear, my weary feet had sped—
> Dark was the night, but at the enchanted dome
>   I saw the infernal windows flaming red.

At last the hour of dissolution arrives:

> Dim burnt the lamp, and now the phantom Death
>   Gave his last groans in horror and despair—
> " All hell demands me hence "— he cried, and threw
>   The red lamp hissing through the midnight air.
>
> Trembling, across the plain my course I held,
>   And found the grave-yard, loitering through the
>   gloom,
> And, in the midst, a hell-red wandering light,
>   Walking in fiery circles round the tomb.

Whereupon with a gruesome picture of Death's
interment and a few stanzas of proper exhortation
from the author, this remarkable poem comes to
an end.

Between the period of the Revolution and the
period that may be called the New England renaissance not much was written which has the distinct mark of the American temperament.   Yet it
is a significant fact that Charles Brockden Brown's

Wieland, published in 1798, the first novel of the
first American novelist, should be built upon a
theme as weird and as steeped in " thrilling melancholy," to use Brown's own words, as anything
in the later work of Hawthorne or Poe; and in
the proper place it would not be uninteresting to
show how far, in his imperfect way, Brown antici-
pates the very methods and tricks of his greater
followers. His immediate inspiration comes no
doubt from the mystery-mongering novels then so
popular in England, but despite the crudeness of
a provincial style there does run through the
strange unreality of Brown's pages a note of sincerity, the tongue and accents of a man to whom
such themes are a native inheritance, lending to
his work a sustained interest which I for my part
fail to find in the *Castle of Otranto* or the *Mysteries
of Udolpho*. Nor is it without significance that
even in New York, where if anywhere this world
claims her own, Irving in his genial way could
fall so easily into brooding on the dead who sleep
in Westminster Abbey or relate with such gusto
the wild legends of the Hudson. Bryant, too, has
kept his fame chiefly on account of his youthful
musings on death and the grandiose pomp of those
lines that tell how the rock-ribbed hills, the pensive vales, the venerable rivers, brooks,

> and, poured around them all,
> Old Ocean's grey and melancholy waste,—
> Are but the solemn decorations all
> Of the great tomb of man.

Necessarily this age-long contemplation of things unearthly, this divorcing of the imagination from the fair and blithe harmonies of life to fasten upon the sombre effects of guilt and reprobation, this constant meditation on death and decay—necessarily all these exerted a powerful influence on literature when the renaissance appeared in New England and as a sort of reflection in the rest of the country. So, I think, it happened that out of that famous group of men who really created American literature the only two to attain perfection of form in the higher field of the imagination were writers whose minds were absorbed by the weirder phenomena of life. But it must not be inferred thence that the spirit of Hawthorne and Poe was identical with that of Michael Wigglesworth and Jonathan Edwards. With the passage of time the unquestioning, unflinching faith and vision of those heroic men dissolved away. Already in Freneau, himself born of a Huguenot family, a change is noticeable; that which to the earlier Fathers was a matter of infinite concern, that which to them was more real and urgent than the breath of life, becomes now chiefly an intoxicant of the imagination, and in another generation the transition is complete.

It is this precisely that we understand by the term "weird"—not the veritable vision of unearthly things, but the peculiar half vision inherited by the soul when faith has waned and the imagination prolongs the old sensations in a shadowy involuntary life of its own; and herein too lies the field of true and effective symbolism. If Hawthorne and Poe, as we think, possess an element of force and realism such as Tieck and the German school utterly lack, it is because they write from the depths of this profound moral experience of their people.

THE INFLUENCE OF EMERSON

IT is a quality of the human spirit on which Emerson himself was wont to dwell, that it forever seeks and knows no rest save in death. Almost it should seem that one cannot acquaint himself with the history of great religions and philosophies without falling at last into a state of wondering indifference or despair, so many times has the truth appeared to men and been formulated for the uplifting of a generation, only to give way in turn to another glimpse of the same haunting reality. We comfort ourselves with the words of the poet whom Emerson loved to quote,— a modern version of Pandora:

> So strength first made a way:
> Then beautie flow'd, then wisdome, honour, pleasure:
> When almost all was out, God made a stay,
> Perceiving that alone of all his treasure
> Rest in the bottome lay. . . .

> For if I should (said he)
> Bestow this jewell also on my creature,
> He would adore my gifts instead of me,
> And rest in Nature, not the God of Nature.
> So both should losers be.

When, therefore, we consider how the wisdom of prophets and philosophers in the past has so swiftly solidified into a formalism that holds the weaker in bondage like a strait jacket, and when we remember how our sage of Concord pointed out that Christianity too must needs fall into "the error that corrupts all attempts to communicate religion," when we reflect on the inevitable course of human thought, those of us who are lovers of Emerson—as I myself am a lover—need feel no grievance to be told that Emersonianism to-day is a sign of limitation, not of strength; of palsy, not of growth. I say Emersonianism, meaning the influence of Emerson as it works on large masses of men; but I would not imply that the individual reader of Emerson may not go to him for ever renewed inspiration and assurance in the things of the spirit. It is always so. The teaching of Plato was as true in the days of the later Academy, is as true now, as it was when Socrates disputed with his disciple in the market-place of Athens; yet almost in the space of a generation Platonism became a snare to those who rest in words and possess no corresponding inner vision of their own. So Emerson cannot escape his own condemnation of the wise: " Though in our lonely hours we draw a new strength out of their memory, yet, pressed on our attention, as they are by the thoughtless and customary, they fatigue and invade."

Only there is a difference to observe. The evil

which has sprung from other systems of thought
has been due chiefly to the very fact that they
were systems and thus attempted to lay restrain-
ing hands on the ever fluent human spirit. Out
of the pursuit of truth has grown a metaphysic;
out of religious faith has developed a theology.
But with Emerson the opposite is true; the mischief that now works in his name is owing in
large part to his very lack of system. Yet it is
but a shallow reader who would go a step further
and accept Emerson's quizzical profession of in-
consistency without reserve. " I would write on
the lintels of the door-post, *Whim*," he said, but
added immediately, "I hope it is somewhat better
than whim at last." His essays ripple and recoil
on the surface, but underneath there is a current
setting steadily to one point. Indeed I have never
been able to understand the minds of those who,
like Richard Garnett, declare that the separate
sentences in Emerson are clear, but that his essays
as a whole are dark because composed without
any central constructive thought and, in fact,
filled with contradictions. It should seem that
critics who find Emerson self-contradictory are
just those who should never have meddled with
him, for the reason that the guiding and formative
principle in all his work is meaningless to them.
Though often capricious in expression and on the
surface illogical, Emerson, more than almost any
other writer of wide influence, displays that inner
logic which springs from the constant insistence

on one or two master ideas. The apparent contradictions in his pages need but a moment's reflection and a modicum of understanding to reduce
them to essential harmony. Like all teachers of
spiritual insight he was profoundly impressed by
the ubiquitous dualism of life. "Philosophically
considered," he wrote in his first famous mani-
festo, "the universe is composed of Nature and
the Soul." I will not stay to show how this
commonplace of thought becomes fruitful of
varied wisdom through the sincerity and depth
of Emerson's vision. I think, in fact, that any-
one who understands with his heart as well as
with his head the central ideas of the essay on the
Oversoul and of that on Experience will need no
such guidance; he possesses a cue that will carry
him like Ariadne's thread through all the laby-
rinth of Emerson's philosophy. Thus of the
Oversoul it is written:

Meantime within man is the soul of the whole; the
wise silence; the universal beauty, to which every part
and particle is related; . . . this deep power in which
we exist, and whose beatitude is all accessible to us, self-
sufficing and perfect in every hour;

and of the Experience of nature it is written:

Dream delivers us to dream, and there is no end to
illusion. Life is a train of moods like a string of beads,
and, as we pass through them, they prove to be many-
coloured lenses which paint the world their own hue,
and each shows only what lies in its own focus.

It is characteristic of Emerson's fine integrity that he never sought—as all systematic philosophies and religions hitherto had attempted — to bridge over the gap between these two realms by a scheme of ratiocination or revelation. He was content to let them lie side by side unreconciled, and hence his seeming fluctuations to those of shallow understanding. In conduct, however, he knew well how to draw the desired lesson from this dilemma. Indeed, I am not sure that all the manifold applications of his genius may not be found summed up in this single paragraph from his later essay on Fate :

> One key, one solution to the mysteries of human condition, one solution to the old knots of fate, freedom and foreknowledge, exists, the propounding, namely, of the double consciousness. A man must ride alternately on the horses of his private and public nature, as the equestrians in the circus throw themselves nimbly from horse to horse, or plant one foot on the back of one, and the other foot on the back of the other. So when a man is the victim of his fate, has sciatica in his loins, and cramp in his mind; a club-foot, and a club in his wit; a sour face, and a selfish temper; a strut in his gait, and a conceit in his affection; or is ground to powder by the vice of his race; he is to rally on his relation to the Universe, which his ruin benefits. Leaving the demon who suffers, he is to take sides with the Deity who secures universal benefit by his pain.

But because Emerson's thought revolves so harmoniously about these two central principles, it does not therefore follow that he has a philoso-

phical system. Not only does he make no attempt to connect them logically, but he is satisfied
to apply now one and now the other of them to
the solution of a thousand minor questions without much order or method. Hence it is that
readers who carry to his essays a sense for ratiocination but no ultimate vision of truth find him
both contradictory and obscure. And as he neg-
lected to mould his own thought into a system,
so he requires of those who come to him no systematic preparation. The truth that Emerson
proclaimed is the old, old commonplace that has
arisen before the minds of sages and prophets
from the beginning of time; but they have each
and all conditioned this truth on some discipline of
the reason or the emotions. They have invari-
ably demanded some propædeutic, some adherence
to a peculiar belief or submission to a divine personality, before the disciple should be carried into
the inner circle of ennobled experiences. With
Plato it was dialectics; with Buddha it was the
four-fold truth and the eight-fold path and a com-
prehension of the twelve-fold wheel of causation;
with Jesus it was Follow me. And in this system
or discipline we seem to discern an authentication
of their high claims. Bound up as we are with
so many petty concerns, so many demands of the
body, blinded by sloth and made callous by the
conflict of so many material powers,—it is hard for
us to accept with more than lip assent this call to
the life of the spirit. These words that the phil-

osophers and prophets utter so glibly—are they
not mere words after all, we ask? Do they signify
any reality of life that a man should barter houses
and land for them? We need assurance that these
ecstasies and these long contents of the spiritual
man are not idle boasts, and so this discipline of
faith we accept readily as a necessary part of the
scheme of salvation. We have not ourselves par-
taken of such blessings, yet we can imagine that
by some extraordinary means, some nimble gym-
nastics of the brain, we might be raised to these
incredible heights. But now comes this Yankee
prophet, offering the same spiritual exaltations
freely and without condition to all. If we may
believe him, a man shall walk out under the open
sky and breathe the sweet influences of the spirit
as cheaply as he inhales the untainted breeze.
The preacher stands at the meeting of the ways
and cries to all that pass by: Ho, ye who are
wrapt in the swaddling clothes of reverence and
obedience, cast aside these trammels and walk up-
right in your own strength. What have we to do
with the sacredness of tradition? No law can be
sacred to us but that of our own nature. Nay, follow the whim of the hour; consistency is the hob-
goblin of little minds. Give me health and a day
and I will make the pomp of emperors ridiculous.

> I am the owner of the sphere,
> Of the seven stars and the solar year,
> Of Cæsar's hand, and Plato's brain,
> Of Lord Christ's heart, and Shakespeare's strain.

And the wonder ot it is that no man whose hearing is not utterly drowned by the clamour of the world can read a page of these essays without recognising that Emerson speaks with an absolute and undeceived sincerity. We remember his confession, that " when a man lives with God, his voice shall be as sweet as the murmur of the brook and the rustle of the corn," and it is with him as

When the harmony of heaven
Soundeth the measures of a lively faith.

Upon the reader, despite himself it may be, there steals something of the pure and noble enthusiasm of the seer, and he knows straightway that the things of the inner life are real.

If this were all it would be well. If his message stood only as a perpetual instigation to the strong and a noble promise to inspired youth, we should have much to say of Emerson and little of Emersonianism. And, in fact, it would be indiscriminating to lay at Emerson's door the whole evil of a faded and vulgarised transcendentalism. He was but one of many; others—some, as Channing, even before his day—had taught the same facility of the spiritual life. Yet in him the movement came to its beautiful flower; we are justified in holding him mainly responsible for the harm that flowed from it, as we honour him for the glory that lay therein. And, alas, even in his own day, the doubtful influence of this fatally easy philosophy began to make itself felt. Hawthorne, the most stalwart observer of all that group, tells us how many bats and owls, which were sometimes mistaken for fowls of angelic feather, were attracted by that beacon light of the spirit. It was moreover impossible, he avows, to dwell in Emerson's vicinity without inhaling more or less the mountain atmosphere of his lofty thought; but in the brains of some people it wrought a singular giddiness. And if Emersonianism was mischievous to weak minds then, what shall we say of its influence in New England to-day—nay, throughout the whole country? For it is rampant in our life; it has wrought in our religion, our politics, and our literature a perilous dizziness of the brain.

There is a mysterious faith abroad in the land, which, however we grudge to say it, is the most serious manifestation of religion discoverable in these days. We call it Christian Science, or faith healing, or what not—the gospel of a certain Mrs. Baker-Eddy; but in reality it does not owe its strength to the teaching of an ignorant woman in New Hampshire. It is a diluted and stale product of Emersonianism, and the parentage, I think, is not difficult to discern. To Emerson, as to Mrs. Baker-Eddy, sin and suffering had no real existence; a man need only open his breast to the random influences of heaven to lead the purely spiritual life. Nor is it correct to say, as some fondly suppose, that Christian Science or Emer-

sonianism has any vital connection with Oriental
mysticism.   True, both Emerson and the sages
of the East taught that spirit was the only reality
and that the world of the body and of evil was a deception.   "Life itself is a bubble and a scepticism
and a sleep within a sleep," said Emerson, and
the Hindu summed up the same thought in his
name for the creator, Mâyâ, illusion.   But there
is a radical difference in their attitude to this
truth.   Though the material world was in one
sense illusion and unreality to the Hindu, yet in
another sense it was tremendously real.   Over the
misery and insufficience of mortal existence he
brooded in a way that to us is inconceivable; we
call him a pessimist, and from our ordinary point
of view rightly.   He was haunted as with an infinite sadness by the vision of endlessly recurring
birth and death, of ceaseless unmeaning mutation.
To escape this life of unspeakable sorrow he la-
boured at vast systems of philosophy, he was
ready to undergo, if needs were, a lifetime of
crushing asceticism.   He could no more have
understood the jaunty optimism of Emerson than
we can understand what we style his pessimism.
There is a story—how authentic I do not know—
that when Emerson was visiting Carlyle, the gruff
Scotchman, who certainly believed heartily in evil
and damnation, carried his guest to the slums of
London and pointed out to him one horrible sight
after another.   "And do you believe in the deil,
noo?" he would say; and always Emerson would

shake his head in gentle denial. The story is at least *ben trovato;* it sets forth clearly the facile optimism out of which Christian Science was to spring. Such a creed, when professed by one who spoke with the noble accent and from the deep insight of an Emerson, was a radiant possession for seeking humanity forever; it is folly and inner deception when repeated parrot-like by men and women with no mental training and, visibly to all the world, with no warrant of spiritual experience. To suppose that you and I and our neighbour can at our sweet will cast off the impediments of sin and suffering is a monstrous self-deceit. So has the very lack of system in Emerson's message become a snare to mankind more deadly than the hardening systems of other philosophies. These are at least virile.

It is at best an ungrateful office to lay bare the harmful influence of a beloved teacher, and I would hurry over what little remains to be said. In politics the unreflecting optimism of transcendental Boston has given birth to that unformed creature called Anti-imperialism. I do not mean such anti-imperialism as would dispute on the grounds of expediency our policy in the Philippines or elsewhere—this is a question of statesmanship — but that " Saturnalia or excess of Faith " which wantonly closes the eyes to distinctions and would see a Washington in every Aguinaldo. It is a blinking of the eyes to those "unconcerning things, matters of fact," in political

6

fitness as Christian Science was in moral fitness; it is the glorification of untried human
nature preached by Channing, made beautiful by
Emerson, acted by the Abolitionists, and reduced
to the absurd by Mr. Atkinson. And the same
optimism has made itself felt in recent New England literature. " The vision of genius comes by
renouncing the too officious activity of the understanding and giving leave and amplest privilege
to the spontaneous sentiment," wrote Emerson;
and again, " The poet must be a rhapsodist, his
inspiration a sort of casualty;" and yet again,
" The Supreme Mind finds itself related to all its
works and will travel a royal road to particular
knowledges and powers;"—excellent doctrine for
a Shakespeare or an Emerson, a noble source of
inspiration for all, indeed; but conceive the havoc
it might work, has indeed actually wrought, when
accepted literally by writers of a single talent. I
was impressed recently by a criticism in the London *Times* which held up to ridicule the cheap
enthusiasms, the utter want of discrimination between inspiration and twaddle, the flaccid sublimi-
ties, of a certain book by Lilian Whiting, which
deals with the literary memories of those old Boston Days. It set me to reflecting on the widespread
mischief done to New England writing of to-day
by this self-abandonment to ecstasy and this easy
acceptance of genius wherever it proclaims itself
—in New England at least. Pessimism is morbid
and stationary, but I sometimes think that the

black hopelessness of a Leopardi would be better than this self-deceit of a facile optimism.

But enough. I feel already something of that shame which must have fallen upon the *advocatus diaboli* constrained by his office to utter a protest against the saints. Yet I trust my words will not be taken as directed against the sweet spirit of Emerson, whom I reverence this side idolatry; I have merely written on the ancient text, *Corruptio optimi pessima.*

P.S.—This essay was published in the *Independent* in connection with the centenary of Emerson's birth, May 25, 1903, and immediately drew from Mrs. Eddy a promulgation setting forth to all the world the extent of her education and denouncing the idea that Christian Science owes anything to Emerson, or to Greek or Roman. She and God alone, it appears, are to be accredited with this new faith. In view of the fact that Mrs. Eddy now numbers her disciples by the million—many of them educated and thoughtful people—we regard this promulgation as one of the most extraordinary documents in the history of religion.

"I was early," she says, "the pupil of Miss Sarah J. Bodwell, the principal of Sanbornton Academy of New Hampshire, and finished my course of studies under Prof. Dyer H. Sanborn, author of Sanborn's Grammar. Among my early studies were Comstock's Natural Philosophy, chemistry, Blair's Rhetoric, Whateley's Logic, Watts's *On the Mind and Moral Science.* At sixteen years of age I began writing for leading newspapers, and for many years wrote for the best magazines in the South and North. I have lectured in large and crowded halls in New York City, Chicago, Boston, Portland, and at

Waterville College, and have been invited to lecture in London and Edinburgh. In 1883 I started the *Christian Science Journal*, and for several years was the proprietor and sole editor of that journal. In 1893 Judge S. J. Hanna became editor of the *Christian Science Journal*, and for ten subsequent years he knew my ability as an editor. In his recent lecture at Chicago, he said: 'Mrs. Eddy is, from every point of view, a woman of sound education and liberal culture' . . .

"I am the author of the Christian Science text book, *Science and Health with Key to the Scriptures*, and the demand for this book increases, and the book is already in its two hundred and seventy-fourth edition of one thousand copies each. I am rated in the *National Magazine* (1903) as 'standing the eighth in a list of twenty-two of the foremost living authors.' "—But withal she is modest. "I claim," she concludes, "no special merit of any kind. All that I am in reality God has made me."

Fatuity has not often gone beyond this. *Tantum religio potuit suadere* ineptiarum.

THE SPIRIT OF CARLYLE

AT last, with the publication of the *New Letters of Thomas Carlyle*,[1] we have a complete survey of his correspondence from the early schoolmaster days when he was teaching mathematics " with some potential outlook on Divinity as ultimatum," to the last waiting years at Chelsea of the acknowledged prophet to whom the final mercy of God seemed that " He delivers us from a life which has become a task too hard." The earlier volumes of the series were edited by Professor Norton, the last two by Carlyle's nephew, both editors being avowedly hostile to Carlyle's biographer, the careless, the much maligned, James Anthony Froude. As for the long quarrel that has been waged between the heirs of Froude and Carlyle, let us hope that this disgraceful chapter in our literary history has been closed, and forever. The most unfortunate episode of this Battle of the Books was the recent publication by his heirs of a pamphlet which had been written by Froude under the influence of that morbid meddler, Miss Geraldine Jewsbury,

[1] *New Letters of Thomas Carlyle.* Edited and annotated by Alexander Carlyle.   2 vols.   New York: John Lane, 1904.

and which contained charges against Carlyle of an astounding and revolting nature. In itself the pamphlet was harmless. No one whose psychological perception was not for the moment deranged could read the early letters of Carlyle to his wife, or indeed follow any part of his career, without being utterly convinced of his virility. But in another sense the pamphlet might have done a great wrong; its silliness and falsehood were of a kind to discredit all that Froude had written about his master, and so to destroy our confidence in one of the two great biographies of the language. We might have been forced to believe that the Life of Carlyle was written by a knave as the Johnson, according to Macaulay, was written by a fool. The work of Froude's enemies has relieved us of this difficulty. By publishing the *Letters* and *Reminiscences* in authentic form they have indeed proved that Froude made innumerable errors in detail, that his methods as an historian were extraordinary, often unaccountable (which, for that matter, was well enough known before), that in some respects he emphasised unwarrantably the harsher side of Carlyle's character; but they have also and unwillingly shown that Froude, despite his blunders, despite the scandal of the recent pamphlet, did succeed nevertheless in writing a biography no less remarkable for its insight into character than for its artistic form. After reading the ten volumes edited by Professor Norton and Mr. Alexander

Carlyle and then turning again to Froude's biography, one may well be impressed by the masterly manner in which that great writer has seized on the real Carlyle, which lies half concealed in the letters, and set him forth in all the clear relief of supreme craftsmanship. The rugged sage of Chelsea looms up as tremendous in English literature as the burly dictator of the earlier century —and it is withal a true picture. It is quite probable that the bulk of Carlyle's work will be little read in the future, as has happened with Johnson; his unflagging vehemence, his determination to seize always on the emotional content of each fact, do certainly render his histories monotonous. But in the record of his life he will continue, like Johnson, to amuse, to instruct, and to dominate. There lives his personality which the world cannot afford to neglect; there, too, speaks the eloquent message of the man. I have thought that it would not be amiss to point out the two peculiar traits of his character whose conjunction, it has seemed to me, accounts for the domination of his spirit over the finer minds of the age, and whose mutual incompatibility brought about the pitiful tragedy of his domestic life.

In part the fascination of Carlyle's character and writings springs from a quality rarely found among Anglo-Saxons, from that sense of illusion which we call Oriental and which is really the basis of Hindu religion. It is a sense far removed from the ordinary bustling practical intelligence

of Britain and America, a form of mysticism, as
we vaguely call it, which is spurned under that
all-comprehensive word un-English or un-Ameri-
can, which yet here and there crops up unaccount-
ably in our greater poets. To Shakespeare, most
of all, the feeling came often with strange effect in
the midst of his stormy passions; and it is not by
chance that Carlyle's favourite quotation was that
outcry of Macbeth at the end of a tumultuous
career : " To-morrow, and To-morrow, and To-
morrow ! " To him, as to Macbeth, life was "but
a walking shadow." Sufficient emphasis has
hardly been laid upon this phase of Carlyle's
mind. Froude must have recognised it in a way,
for the selections he makes use of from the letters
and journals are filled with the sense of spectral
vision, yet nowhere does he point out definitely the
kinship between his master and those eremites
of ancient India who, in pursuit of that great
silence which Carlyle preached so vociferously,
withdrew for meditation to the solitary groves and
mountain caves. Not Bhartrihari himself, the
philosopher king of Oujjein, was more haunted
by the bewildering phantasmagoric aspect of the
world than this peasant-born son of Ecclefechan.
Life in well-ordered England was to Carlyle a
struggle with " the whirlwind and wild piping
battle of fate." Everywhere it was the same;
whether at Craigenputtock or by the weltering
sea or in the roaring streets of London, he was
awed by the noisy insignificance of the world

swimming through the void of space, by the
frantic unrest of the heart of man looking out
upon the eternal repose of the hills, by the clamorous discord of human life beneath the great
silences of the sky; everywhere he moved among
spectres and illusions.   Walking at night over the
moors about his Craigenputtock home, he found
it "silent, solitary as Tadmor in the wilderness;
yet the infinite vault still over it, and the earth a
little ship of space in which he was sailing."
Later in life he visits the old birthplace at Ecclefechan, and there on the road sits for a while
alone, looking across to the Cumberland mountains and calling up the shadows of the past.
"Tartarus itself," he said, "and the pale king-
doms of Dis, could not have been more preter-
natural to me—most stern, gloomy, sad, grand
yet terrible, yet steeped in woe."   More often
amid the solemn scenes of nature the illusion of
man's discordant fate sank away beneath the
brooding presence of the infinite.   Very beautiful
in feeling is the passage quoted by Froude from a
letter written at Linlathen: "Yesternight, before
sunset, I walked solitary to Stockbridge hilltop,
the loneliest road in all Britain, where you go and
come some three miles without meeting a human
soul.   Strange, earnest light lay upon the moun-
tain-tops all round, strange clearness; solitude as
if personified upon the near bare hills, a silence
everywhere as if premonitory of the grand eternal
one."   Was he thinking of Goethe's "Ueber allen

Gipfeln ist Ruh," when he wrote? That may not
be known, but one thing is certain: It is because
Froude had the wisdom to build up his biography
on such excerpts as this that it presents a true
and momentous portrait of the man; and con-
versely it is because Mr. Alexander Carlyle omits
this letter and others like it (they were written
during a period of estrangement between Carlyle
and his wife) that his collection is of secondary
interest, and really belittles the man he attempts
to magnify.

But it was in London Carlyle felt the inscrutable mystery of life weigh upon him as a hideous
nightmare.   There the world looked " often quite
spectral " to him.   " It is and continues a wild
wondrous chaotic den of discord, this London,"
he writes.   " I am often wae and awestruck at
once to wander along its crowded streets, and see
and hear the roaring torrent of men and animals
and carriages and wagons, all rushing they know
not whence, they know not whither!"   It is not
strange that he often felt himself " the loneliest of
all the sons of Adam," or that " in the jargon of
poor grimacing men" he seemed to listen " to the
jabbering of spectres."   One day, while the spirit
of the French Revolution is upon him, he calls at
Mrs. Austin's, where he hears " Sydney Smith
for the first time guffawing, other persons prating,
jargoning."   He writes of it in his journal, and
adds: "*To me through these thin cobwebs Death
and Eternity sate glaring.*"   Often, as I read of

Carlyle and reflect how life to him was a perilous
journey through phantoms and fiery thronging
illusions, I recall passages of the Hindu books,
and one epigram in particular comes to my mind:

> Seated within this body's car
> The silent Self is driven afar;
> And the five senses at the pole
> Like steeds are tugging, restive of control.
>
> And if the driver lose his way,
> Or the reins sunder, who can say
> In what blind paths, what pits of fear
> Will plunge the chargers in their mad career?

And in another way Carlyle was filled with the
Oriental spirit. To him, as to the philosophers
of India, only one fact was certain in this ever-
shifting mirage of our worldly life. Running
through it all was the unvarying moral law of
cause and effect: what a man sowed that should
he inevitably reap. It is not necessary to dwell
on this point, for no one can read a page of Carlyle's writings without learning that the very
warp and woof of his doctrine were the tremendous certainty of virtue and vice, of the retributive
law of justice. Sometimes he expresses this sense
of the indwelling reality in the old terms of God
and Providence which he had inherited in his
Scottish home; at other times he speaks in the
more mystical manner of the East, as if an impersonal law of morality wrought within us and

created our destiny. In that passage quoted
above, in which he describes the bewildering
phantasmagoria of the London streets, he adds:
"Nevertheless, there *is* a deep, divine meaning
in it, and God is in the midst of it, had we but
eyes to see." And elsewhere a thousand times
in his letters and formal works he expresses the
same sentiment. Here alone lay the lesson and
significance of history, in the terrible assurance
of retribution following hard upon transgression
of the ten commandments. "All history is a
Bible," he says, and adds somewhat plaintively
that he has preached this solemn doctrine through
a lifetime, but only to deaf ears. This it was that
made the French Revolution, to his mind, the
most significant event in human affairs; others
saw in that catastrophe the awakening of liberty;
Carlyle beheld only a stern Providence dealing
retribution to a sinful people. "I should not have
known what to make of this world at all," he
ejaculates, "if it had not been for the French
Revolution." And his history of that upheaval
is nothing other than a lyric rhapsody over the
illusion of life, the cant and mockery of words,
pierced through and through by the wrath of the
divine reality. The men and women of his pages
are spectres hounded by the loud Furies. The
vision of the whole is as it were pictures of fire
thrown on a curtain of seething cloud. In a letter
to Thomas Erskine (which, it may be noted, is
not included in the collection made by Mr. Alex-

ander Carlyle) he sums up the truth which he felt
it his mission to preach:

The great soul of this world is Just. With a voice soft
as the harmony of the spheres, yet stronger, sterner, than
all thunders, this message does now and then reach us
through the hollow jargon of things. This great fact we
live in, and were made by.

Nor was his attitude toward the individual in
any way different from his understanding of history. For himself he seemed to be swathed and
" embated " in enchantments from which no man
could deliver him until death freed him once for
all. " One thing in the midst of this chaos," he
writes, "I can more and more determine to adhere
to—it is now almost my sole rule of life—to clear
myself of cants and formulas as of poisonous
Nessus shirts; to strip them off me, by what name
soever called, and follow, were it down to Hades,
what I myself know and see." And several times
he recurs to this conception of himself as a weary
Hercules, struggling with the venomed shirts of
illusion that wrapt his soul about. Here, too, lies
the explanation of his much-reiterated doctrine of
work. He first, apparently got the lesson from
Goethe, to whom work was a kind of glorified
prudential means of attaining happiness and self-
development, but soon carried it into a region
quite beyond the great German's range of vision.
In the midst of innumerable mockeries and deceptions he perceived one absolute certainty — that

the deeds of man wove influences about him which
were the creation of his destiny. This was the
law of justice that remained steadfast, though all
the religious imaginings of Jew and Gentile were
swept away, and Jove and Jehovah faded into
oblivion. Through all his doubts he proclaimed
this mystic gospel of Work with appalling vocif-
eration. One is reminded again of the creed of
those philosophers of India to whom Carlyle in so
many ways bore a strangely distorted likeness.
From the preacher of London shouting his message through the din of our Western civilisation, I
turn to Bhartrihari and read his quaint epigrams,
written, we may suppose, after he had retired from
the throne and sought the silence and seclusion of
his cavern dwelling beyond the houses of Oujjein:

> Before the Gods we bend in awe,
> But lo, they bow to fate's dread law:
> Honour to Fate, then austere lord!
> But lo, it fashions but our works' reward.
>
> Nay, if past works our present state
> Engender, what of gods and fate?
> Honour to Works! in them the power
> Before whose awful nod even fate must cower.

No wonder that with such a burden to deliver
Carlyle found himself like one crying in the wilderness. Men listened and were startled from their
lethargy; they honoured him with the name of
prophet, and gaped upon him with a vague dread,
but in the end they shook their heads and turned

away as from an inspired madman. It may be that the message of Carlyle was the old truth of the sages announced in a new and astounding form; certainly it was in every way diametrically opposed to the current of belief that swept through the nineteenth century. Those were the days when science was reaching forth to usurp the kingdom of thought. Evolution announced that the material world alone was governed by immutable and discoverable laws, and that morality was based on the ever-shifting quicksands of custom and tradition; Carlyle perceived in the phenomena of life only thin cobwebs, wherethrough Death and Eternity sate glaring, whereas the moral law alone was unchangeable, founded on the everlasting rock of truth. As a people we have entrusted our destiny to Darwin and Spencer and Huxley, and to Carlyle we have granted the dubious praise of having written *Literature!* Nor was he in any closer sympathy with the religious aims of the day. That was the time, on the one hand, of Puseyism and the Oxford movement which undertook to counteract the scepticism of science by an appeal to tradition and the influence of imaginative symbols, and, on the other hand, of the strenuous religion of Maurice and Kingsley, who sought to smother doubts in restless activity. Towards both movements Carlyle was perfectly cold, even scornful. These good men seemed to him to be deliberately forging self-deceptions to take the place of the old faith, and his answer to their challenge

was a fierce proclamation of " the Exodus from
Houndsditch." In politics he was, if possible,
still more opposed to the current of the age. Democracy was then gathering up her strength for
the long and apparently victorious struggle with
inherited powers and principalities. The ballot
box was to be the guarantee of righteous government, and the will of the majority was in all
things to rule supreme. Carlyle believed that the
multitude of men were blinded with the illusions
of this world, and that to trust to their judgment
was like leaving the guidance of a rudderless
vessel to the waves of the sea. He would stand
neither with Radicals nor Tories. To the former
he preached the instability of all mobs; to the latter he pointed out the sufferings of the poor, and
the idle, fox-hunting habits of the aristocracy.
He saw salvation for the people only where a
strong man ruled by right of the divine reality
speaking through him. When asked who was to
determine whether the strong man was the good
man, whether might was right, he exclaimed sav-
agely that hell-fire would be the judge, as it had
already judged in the French Revolution.

In every dispute the world, after its ancient
manner, decided against him in its own favour.
It would not be easy to name a single great question or tendency of the age which was in any way
guided or balked by his vehement prophesying.
If his influence was deep and undeniable, it was
due to that curious dualism that exists in most

of us between our public and our private conscience. Men listened to his social denunciations
with amazement or with mockery; there was no
room for his mysticism in the spirit of compromise
and utilitarianism that governed, and no doubt
must always govern, public affairs. But in private, when the individual man turned from the
clamour of opinions to meditate in the secret
chamber of his thought, then the words of Carlyle
penetrated to the heart with the authority of that
voice, still and small, yet stronger, sterner than
all thunders, that none shall hear and with impunity disobey. To those who are absorbed in
the philosophy of this world Carlyle's doctrine has
had no meaning and probably will never have a
meaning ; to one who reflects apart and seeks a
solitary law for his own guidance, Carlyle will
long remain, as he stands revealed in Froude's
pages, a revered friend and a dreaded mentor.

The wonder is not that Carlyle's political and
religious theories went unheeded, but that he
himself received publicly such honour in the land
as a prophet. That is a paradox which sprang
from a contradiction in his own nature. He compelled men to listen to him by that strange union
of qualities which was at once his strength and
his weakness. His preaching in part was not unlike the philosophy of those Indian gymnosophists
who from Alexander's day to ours have been a
marvel and a disturbing doubt to the Occident.
But to the Hindus' belief in the illusion of life and

7

in the mystic dominion of Works, he added an emotional consciousness utterly foreign to their temper. This was an exaggerated and highly irritable sense of his individual personality. Now the personal character of a man, as we of the West understand it, was to the Hindu a transitory composite, a mere aspect of the general illusion; while the Hebrew, with his purely concrete intelligence, carried the idea into the very heavens, and made of his Jehovah the most intense personality the human brain has ever conceived. The combination of these two ways of viewing the world, the outer sense of illusion joined to an aggravated self-consciousness, gave that peculiar poignancy to Carlyle's preaching which we all feel, but do not always stop to analyse. Never before perhaps has the world listened to the mystic philosophy of illusion thundered forth with the virulence and tremendous vehemence of a Jeremiah or an Ezekiel. It was, of course, the Hebrew element in his character that impressed and for a while cowed his British audience; it was the Hindu mysticism that rendered his doctrine utterly unavailing in the end to influence the current of public opinion.

If this self-contradiction of Carlyle's views created the singular paradox of a prophet publicly feared but unheeded, it wrought only disaster in his domestic life. I think one need not go beyond this union of warring traits to comprehend the tumult of Carlyle's own conscience and the more pathetic tragedy of his marriage. We can easily believe him when he says he is no man " whom it is desirable to be too close to." He moved in a nightmare of fantastic unrealities and heard only the "jabbering of spectres," but with his exacerbated egotism he could not wave them aside as mere shadows, and rise to the calm of that higher self which can smile unconcerned at the idle illusion. He was among them and of them; they beat upon his brain and tortured his nerves, until he cried out like a bewildered, much-buffeted Titan. "My heart," he exclaimed, "is burnt with fury and indignation when I think of being cramped and shackled and tormented as never man till me was." The very trivialities of life must loom up tremendously, like the distorted images seen through a mist. The very beasts and dumb things of the earth became a part of the infernal Walpurgis Night that weltered about him, and the human beings that thwarted him were emissaries of Satan. When he hears a watchman in Edinburgh proclaim the passing of the hours, the man is transformed into a demon. " There was one of those guardians there," he says in a letter, " whose throat I could have cut that night; his voice was loud, hideous, and ear and soul piercing, resembling the voices of ten thousand gib-cats all molten into one terrific peal." He travels in Germany, and the beds wring a scream from him like that of a man broken on the rack. His warfare against his neighbour's cocks has become a part of history, and when workmen entered his Chelsea house he fled as if the horrors of the Inferno had broken in upon him. There is, of course, an element of humorous exaggeration in his complaints; grim, stentorian humour was indeed the natural product of a brain so strangely and contradictorily compacted. But to himself and to his wife the merriment must have sounded too often like the reputed laughter of the pit. "Ah me! People ought not to be angry at me," he writes in a letter to Jane. " People ought to let me alone. Perhaps they would if they rightly understood what I was doing and suffering in this Life Pilgrimage at times."

It is folly to-day to enter into that domestic unhappiness and take sides for one or the other of the sufferers; if we rightly understand Carlyle there will be no room left for anger; nor, on the other hand, shall we attempt to transfer the blame of the unhappiness wholly from his shoulders to hers. It is well to remember, also, how often the demonic nature of the world and of his own tortured personality sank away and left him at peace; how often the illusion of life detached itself from his own morbid egotism and appeared as a scene of infinite pathos, a matter for tears and not for execrations. At these times his heart went out in tenderness, and his letters to Jane and to others are filled with exquisite love and simple sweetness such as no other letters of the language can parallel. If we were compelled to select a single passage which showed the real character of the man, with its depth and brooding insight, we might well quote these words, which he wrote to his brother John:

Last night I sat down to smoke in my nightshirt in the back yard. It was one of the beautifullest nights; the half-moon, clear as silver looked out as from eternity, and the great dawn was streaming up. I felt a remorse, a kind of shudder, at the fuss I was making about a sleepless night, about my sorrow at all, with a life so soon to be absorbed into the great mystery above and around me. Oh! let us be patient. Let us call to God with our silent hearts, if we cannot with our tongues.

There the unrest of his soul dies away and the clear serenity of the philosopher speaks out.

I have thus attempted to find a key to the peculiar paradox of Carlyle's life and writings in the extraordinary union within one man of the spirit of the Hindu seer and the Hebrew prophet —although of direct influence from India there is, of course, no suggestion intended. It would not be difficult, indeed, to show that something of this paradoxical temperament is inherent in the Scotch character, and that Carlyle inherited it from his people and his surroundings as he acquired the remarkable qualities of his style. The transition from the pages of such writers as John Knox and Rutherford and Peden and Hutcheson to his own consummate eloquence is less marked than might commonly be supposed.

But beyond such inheritance lies the genius of the man himself, the mystery of his brain, which no study of tradition or acquisition will explain.   He stands in Froude's biography a figure unique, isolated, domineering—after Dr. Johnson the greatest personality in English letters, possibly even more imposing than that acknowledged dictator.

THE SCIENCE OF ENGLISH VERSE

MR. MARK H. LIDDELL, formerly of the University of Texas, has written a little book [1] on the scientific study of English poetry which is not without interesting suggestions. It is a pity, however, that he should have adopted a tone of such revolutionary violence as is likely to discredit what is really valuable in his work. There were brave men before Agamemnon's time, and there have been "scientific" students of verse even before this present year of grace. And is it quite prudent for a writer on a subject which has been treated by a succession of sincere scholars through many centuries to assert so frankly, whatever his secret thoughts may be, that all who preceded him were mere indulgers in empty metaphysics, silly idolaters before those awful *idola* of error which Bacon discovered and laid bare in the market-place and elsewhere? "The conclusion of the whole matter," says Mr. Liddell at the end of his treatise, "points but in one direction—the

[1] *An Introduction to the Scientific Study of English Poetry.* By Mark H. Liddell. New York: Doubleday, Page & Co. 1902.

necessity of considering literature as material of science, and not as a subject for pleasant talk.''

Now Mr. Liddell's consideration of literature as material of science is divided into two parts, the first having to do with a general discussion of the elements of poetry, the second being confined more exclusively to rhythm in verse. In summing up the argument of the first part he expresses himself as follows (p. 140):

The general notion of poetry we thus obtained was: ideas normally formulated in the terms of correlated sound-group-images, possessing the general and abiding human interest of literature, and rendered æsthetically interesting by being couched in recognisably æsthetic Verse Form. Or, stated as a formula: $x + \mathrm{HI} + \mathrm{VF}$.

Evidently the author has been at some pains to avoid '' pleasant talk'' and to be strictly scientific. He lets x stand for the underlying idea of the poem, HI for its human interest, and VF for its verse form. A poem, in other words, must contain some thought or idea expressed in normal language; it must further possess some general human interest; and it must be in verse form. Why, of course; we all know that. M. Jourdain, in the play, was amazed to learn that he had been speaking prose all his life; on translating Mr. Liddell's formula we are flattered to find that we have been thinking, if not speaking, science all along without ever suspecting it. The pity of it is that our dulness should have required one hundred and forty pages of strenuous argument to receive such enlightenment. And, seriously, is it not regrettable that jargon of this kind should be allowed to drown some really clever bits of criticism? For instance, the contrast instituted (p. 30 ff.) between Shakespeare's " After life's fitful fever he sleeps well " and the same thought in prose form, is neatly done and is interesting, though it may contain nothing that borders on revolutionary originality.

But it is the second part of the book which forms the heart of Mr. Liddell's argument; and if I have seemed to dwell at too great length on the introductory matter, it was in the desire to set forth the peculiar tone that has crept into the scientific discussion of rhythm from various literary sources. It is in this second part that the author pours out the vials of his wrath against his predecessors who were reckless enough to contradict him by anticipation. Indeed, the desired dispassionateness of scientific research is more than once broken in these pages by a recrudescence of the old and rancorous debate between the ancients and the moderns. That debate was amusing when Swift sent forth his *Battle of the Books;* it is hardly amusing to-day. And then it is so likely to carry a man away from calm investigation into dreary outbreaks of the *odium philologicum.* Any one not blinded by this malign disease might see, you would suppose, that the contestants on both sides are equally

wrong-headed—both those who frenetically deny
any similarity between classic and English
rhythms, and those who obstinately uphold their
complete identity.

As for the upcropping of this *odium philologicum*
in the present treatise, one wonders a little at the
wherefore.   Part of its animus, no doubt, is due
to the author's inadequate knowledge of the
classics.   For instance, a very little reading would
have prevented such a categorical statement as
this (p. 112), " But [in contrast to the English]
there is ample evidence to show that an absolute
and fixed proportion [between long and short
syllables] did exist in the classic languages; " or
this (p. 65), " We shall look in vain in Greek
poetry for an æsthetic appeal based upon varia-
tions of intensity of syllables."   Aristoxenus,
more than two thousand years ago, exposed the
folly of that first error; and as for the second, the
weight of evidence is strongly in favour of sup-
posing that the feet in a Greek verse were marked
off by a slight " intensity of syllables."   That (p.
26) the author speaks disparagingly of the "vatus
insanus," we would willingly charge to negligent
proof-reading were it not that elsewhere (p. 294)
he, though a professed student of Shakespeare,
misquotes the bard so as to achieve the rhythm,
" O nymph, in thy o-*ri*-sons."

But in part Mr. Liddell's celestial ire against
the classics is justified by the infinite confusion
wrought in English prosody by the ill-advised

critics, from Gabriel Harvey down, who have
failed to distinguish between the nature of quantitative measure in Greek and in the Teutonic
languages. So irritating is this confusion to Mr.
Liddell's Anglo-Saxon sensibilities that he goes
to the other extreme, and denies that the length
or shortness of an English syllable has anything
whatsoever to do with the forms of English verse
—although he does elsewhere admit grudgingly
the existence of quantitative distinctions in English pronunciation. Rhythm, he thinks, is in no-
wise determined by the measurement of time but
by the counting off of accented and unaccented
syllables. Just why he should involve this in-
complete and often exploded theory in such a fury
of hard language, it is not easy to say. Perhaps
he deems it scientific to be obscure. "We have
determined," he writes in conclusion (p. 310),
"that the fundamental element of our English
verse-punctuation is that concomitant of ideation
which we have called attention-stress." This is
a "scientific" (it seems rather metaphysic) statement which may be interpreted to the merely
literary by explaining that "verse-punctuation"
means feet; that "attention-stress" means stress
or accent, which of course catches the attention;
and that "concomitant of ideation" implies that
the accent is governed by the thought. To
such a pass has the *odium philologicum* brought
us!

The wonder of it all is that so simple a matter

as verse-rhythm should have raised so noisy a
commotion.   I am myself tempted to discuss the
subject briefly, affecting some assurance of tone
not because I hope to introduce scientific accuracy
where hitherto empty rhetoric has reigned supreme, but contrariwise because the whole subject
has already received such adequate treatment by
others.   From three readily accessible books one
may learn all that is essential to English prosody
— *The Science of English Verse*, by Sidney Lanier;
Chapters on Greek Metric, by T. W. Goodell; and
Englische Metrik, by J. Schipper.   Lanier's brilliant work is unexceptionable as a study of the
ideal or *model* verse, but fails to consider the variance between the *ideal* and the *actual* rhythm.   A
large part of Prof. Goodell's volume deals with
this very question, and thus supplements Lanier's
theory.   Prof. Goodell is concerned primarily
with Greek rhythms, but in his third chapter he
gives the clearest and sanest discussion of rhythm
in general that I have yet seen—and to my sorrow
I have read much on the subject.   Dr. Schipper's
volumes form a work of vast *Gelehrsamkeit* and
are invaluable as a storehouse of material.

But as a text for my explanation I choose rather
to take the statement of one who certainly cannot
be accused of deficient science, of one who is indeed recognised by the scientific world as the
highest possible authority in all questions of
sound.   In Helmholtz's *Tonempfindungen* these
words may be found (Ellis's Translation, p. 388):

The scientific, as well as all other measurement of time, depends on the rhythmical recurrence of similar events, the revolution of the earth or moon, or the swings of a pendulum. Thus also the regular alternation of accentuated and unaccentuated sounds in music and poetry gives the measure of time for the composition. But whereas in poetry the construction of the verse serves only to reduce the external accidents of linguistic expression to artistic order; in music, rhythm, as the measure of time, belongs to the inmost nature of expression. Hence also a much more delicate and elaborate development of rhythm was required in music than in verse.

From this genuinely scientific statement the three laws of verse-rhythm may be formulated as follows:

I. Rhythm in verse is not the product of either classical or Anglo-Saxon pedantry, but is a branch of acoustics and is amenable to the great rhythmic law of nature.

II. Rhythm in verse, like all rhythm, is a measurement of time marked off by the regular recurrence of similar events.

III. Rhythm in verse is a mere approximation, much less absolute and regular than rhythm in music, which is nearest akin to it.

Let us examine these three laws in order.

I. First of all, then, rhythm in verse is a branch of the scientific study of sound, and has nothing to do with grammar or logic or numbers or thought. It is as amenable to law as any other phenomenon within the realm of acoustics. To speak of rhythm in numbers or the rhythm of thought is a mere metaphorical use of words, an introduction of metaphysics where science should reign. Rhythm may be an instrument to express thought or emotion, and in this way thought or emotion may govern rhythm; but the rhythm remains as distinct from the thought or emotion as the swaying of our limbs from the nerve impulse that moves them. Rhythm is purely a matter of the senses. Doggerel verses which convey no meaning may still be highly rhythmical.

II. Now every appeal to the senses must be some act of energy perceived through the media of space and time. Symmetry has to do with phenomena as determined in space; rhythm, with phenomena as determined in time. To distinguish: Suppose a man at a blackboard to be drawing a continuous line. If this line in the end produces a regularly repeated figure, the design is symmetrical. The time of the drawing and the rapidity of the man's movements are not here concerned. If, however, the figure traced be without design, but if the drawer at regular intervals of time makes some peculiar and repeated movement with his hand, then the resulting figure drawn will not be symmetrical, but the motion of the drawer's hand while drawing will be rhythmical. Symmetry is static, rhythm is kinetic.

The commonest form of rhythm is, of course, the rhythm of sound. And here let it be noted that such rhythm is not a mere division of time (which would be a metaphysical conception), but a division of sound in time. To illustrate: A succession of perfectly similar sounds at regular intervals of time is not rhythmical. There is inherently no rhythm in a succession of equal drum beats at intervals of a second, or in a regular succession of indistinguishable whistles. To produce rhythm, you must mark off certain sounds so as to divide the series into groups occupying equal measures of time. For example, there is rhythm in the drum beats to which we march; there would be rhythm in a succession of whistles such as an engine emits on approaching a road.

There are three properties of sound which may be so used in marking off these groups. At regular intervals of time the sound may be distinguished from the others (1) by duration, or (2) by pitch, or (3) by stress or loudness. The first rhythm would undoubtedly be the weakest, the third would be the strongest. Any combination would be still stronger, as tending to mark off the intervals of time more emphatically to the ear.

Now this rhythmic sense is one of the most insistent in human nature, so insistent that, given any regular succession of sounds, it produces the illusion of rhythm when none actually exists. For instance, it is impossible to listen to the ticking of a clock without imagining some difference between the alternate strokes such as will mark off the sounds into rhythmic groups. Every other stroke seems to be at once a little longer, a little higher in pitch, and louder—tic tác, tic tác, tic tác, etc. That this difference of sound is imaginary becomes evident from the ease with which we may vary the succession at will. The conclusion is this: Rhythm exists only when some diversity of sound marks off regular intervals of time within each of which some sound occurs.

The application of this law to language is perfectly simple. Here the equal measurement of time is determined: (1) by the regular recurrence of syllables distinguished in length, in which case the rhythm may be called quantitative ; (2) by the regular recurrence of syllables distinguished in pitch, in which case the rhythm may be called melodic; (3) by the regular recurrence of syllables distinguished in stress, in which case the rhythm may be called accentual. The practice of languages may vary among these three forms ; but in all languages, where rhythm exists at all, the fundamental law of rhythm must be observed,— there must be a periodic measurement of time. The tedious battle of the books is due to the fact that certain scholars, blinded by their classical predilections, emphasise the fundamental similarity of rhythm in all languages (in the classics and English, specifically), but fail to recognise the accidental varieties; whereas certain other scholars, influenced like Mr. Liddell by their Teutonic studies, consider the accidental variation alone and are ill disposed to acknowledge any fundamental similarity. As a matter of fact, to make such a logomachy more inane, the rhythmic division of time in both Greek and English was probably marked by the same combination of the first and third manners—was at once, that is, quantitative and accentual. Only there is this distinction (which explains if it does not justify the dispute), that in Greek quantitative rhythm was strongly predominant, so much so that some scholars deny the presence of accentual rhythm at all, whereas in English accentual rhythm is predominant. Thus iambic rhythm in Greek is a series of equal measures of time, each measure containing a short syllable followed by a much longer syllable; but it is also practically certain that the long syllables were, as a rule, further marked by a slight stress accent. In English this iambic rhythm is a series of equal measures of time, each containing an unaccented syllable followed by a strongly accented syllable; but it is further true that the accented syllable tends, although not inevitably, to become slightly longer than the unaccented syllable. It is therefore proper to call Greek rhythm quantitative and English rhythm accentual. It is, however, an absurdity to say that the length of syllables has nothing to do with English rhythm. The order of quantities within the feet may sometimes vary, but the quantity of the combined syllables within each foot must be such as to divide the verse into measures of equal time, exactly as music is divided into bars.

8

Quantity is indeed the root of the whole debate, and it may be well to insist on the question a little more. The discussion has arisen from a misunderstanding of quantity in both the classics and English. The quantity of a Greek syllable is determined by fixed laws of pronunciation and is always the same, and, further, a long syllable is reckoned as occupying twice the time of a short; hence quantitative rhythm in Greek assumes the simplicity of an arithmetical ratio. In English, on the other hand, neither of these laws holds good; hence the *non sequitur*, because English quantity does not follow the laws of Greek quantity therefore there is no quantity at all in English. But, unless one is willing to assert that such a syllable as *bursts* is not longer in pronunciation than *at*, it is folly to deny the existence of quantity in English. Only it remains true that quantity in English, while fixed by the laws of enunciation in some syllables, varies in other syllables according to their emphasis in the sentence. And, further, the scheme by which a long syllable in Greek is reckoned as double a short syllable is —and was so recognised by the most authoritative of Greek metricians—a mere fiction of the grammarians to simplify the schematisation of rhythms. If Mr. Liddell, and others who accept literally this ideal schematisation, should reflect a moment (not to mention the profit of reading the authorities on the subject), they would see that no language is or ever was pronounced with such wooden regularity. It is only true to say that the difference in Greek between long and short syllables, though varying, was very decided, and approximated roughly the ratio of 2 to 1. In English the difference in quantity is ordinarily much less than in Greek, but to assert that quantity has no function in English rhythm because English quantities do not have the Greek ratio of 2 to 1, is to fall into a double and really unpardonable error.

A concrete comparison will throw light on the confusion. The first verse of the *Odyssey* reads and is scanned as follows:

Andra moi	ennepe	mousa po-	lytropon	hos
´ ◡ ◡	´ — ◡ ◡	´ — ◡ ◡	´ — ◡ ◡	´ —

mala	polla
◡ ◡	´ — —

The first verse of *Evangeline* is scanned:

This is the	forest pri-	meval the	murmuring	pines
´ — ◡ ◡	´ — ◡ ◡	´ — ◡ ◡	´ — ◡ ◡	´ —

and the	hemlocks
◡ ◡	´ — —

Now it will be observed that these two hexameters are essentially the same. They both consist of six equal measures of time, each measure normally containing one long accented syllable

followed either by two short unaccented syllables
or by one long unaccented syllable. But in their
secondary characteristics the two verses differ
considerably. In the Greek verse the initial long
syllables are much longer than the short syllables,
are in fact approximately equal to the time of the
two short syllables taken together. They are
thus sufficiently distinct to mark off the measures
by their quantitative value. But these initial
syllables have also a slight stress accent, which is
the pure result of the inherent rhythmising instinct of the human mind. This rhythmical stress
is made possible by the fact that Greek words in
normal prose enunciation possess no regular stress
accent at all such as English words possess. In
the English verse, on the contrary, the initial
syllables all have a normal stress due to the
regular verbal or sentence accent, and this stress
is reënforced by the rhythmising instinct. Hence
the accent alone is sufficient to mark off the measures, and it is possible for the arrangement of the
quantities within a measure to vary considerably,
provided only that the sum of the quantities remains fixed. In the foot " pines and the " the
first syllable is approximately the length of the
two following syllables together; in the foot "this
is the," however, the three syllables are about
the same; and between these two extremes every
shade of difference may exist. Only it will be
found a pretty constant rule that the first syllable
is slightly longer than the others if there are three

in the foot, and a still more constant rule that the measures of the verse consist in full of equivalent periods of time. There is quantity in both Greek and English, but it is quite proper to designate the Greek verse as primarily quantitative, and the English verse as primarily accentual.

I have as yet said nothing of the pitch accent, for the reason that the subject is one of some obscurity. It is, however, almost certain that the regular accent of a Greek word was a pitch accent, as distinguished from the English stress accent. It did not fall necessarily on the same syllable with the rhythmical stress accent, and produced thus something of the effect of melody in the recitation of Greek verse. In English this pitch accent is a more complicated question. It plays a little-recognised part in the function of rhythm, but my own observation leads me to believe that it is often used to mark off the time measurement, when the stress accent, by some apparent irregularity of construction, does not correspond to the rhythmic divisions.

III. But all this has to do with the ideal or model rhythm, and we have still to consider the third law derived from Helmholtz's statement—a law so important that the neglect of it in Sidney Lanier's treatise vitiates to a certain extent that poet's brilliant theory. In the actual reading of poetry two distinct, even contradictory, impulses will be found at work—the rhythmising instinct and the normal unrhythmical enunciation of the language. The result is a compromise shifting toward one extreme or the other.

As for the rhythmising instinct in verse, that is merely one clause of a law which runs through every manifestation of energy, of a law so universal that it would appear as if the great heart of nature beat with a regular systole and diastole, sending impulses of rhythmic motion through every artery of the world. So strong is this instinct in us that a child in reading verse falls unconsciously into a monotonous, undeviating singsong which without hesitation sacrifices sense and ordinary pronunciation. When a child recites his *Mother Goose*, you may beat time to his words as easily as you beat time to a dance tune. The process of adapting the ordinary pronunciation of language to this rhythmic impulse is called *plasma*, and was observed by the Greek metricians long ago, as it may readily be observed by us to-day. By *plasma* we lengthen a syllable here and shorten a syllable there, so as to get the exact measure of time within a foot, and where lengthening is not sufficient we insert a pause corresponding precisely in its rhythmical effect to the pauses in music. How exact the rhythm may be made through *plasma* is exemplified in the curious game of " Pease porridge hot," as I was taught it, or " Bean porridge hot," as Professor Goodell calls it, from a Yankee boyhood presumably. I shall not attempt to explain— what every one must have learned as a child—the manner in which the recitation of these words is accompanied by a play of the hands which marks off the rhythm with absolute regularity.

> Pease porridge hot
> Pease porridge cold
> Pease porridge in the pot
> Nine days old.

So the words run, and the rhythm falls into this precise scheme, the macron representing twice the time of a breve, and an inverted v representing a pause equal in length to a breve:

$$\bar{\ } \smile \smile \mid \bar{\ } \wedge \wedge \mid$$
$$\bar{\ } \smile \smile \mid \bar{\ } \wedge \wedge \mid$$
$$\bar{\ } \smile \smile \mid \breve{\ } \smile \smile \wedge \mid$$
$$\bar{\ } \_ \mid \bar{\ } \wedge \wedge \mid$$

The result, however, of giving this rhythmising instinct full play is to render our reading intolerably monotonous and to sacrifice the sense to meaningless sound. The ordinary teacher in our schools, seeing this deplorable effect, drills his pupils to avoid this instinct and to read verse "just as if it were prose." As a consequence, most men, being neither natural nor educated, but only half-educated, do indeed read verse as if it were prose, succeeding so admirably that the

rhythm is lost altogether. For it must be observed that the normal pronunciation of language
does not produce any such regular rhythm as the
poet has before him in mind when he composes.
Verse differs from prose in this: that in verse the
words are so ordered that their normal pronunciation approximates closely enough to a rhythmical
scheme to permit the rhythmising instinct by
means of *plasma* to produce a distinguishable
rhythm without doing great violence to the sense.
Hence no arrangement of words is really rhythmical to the half-educated ear which through
false training resists the rhythmising instinct.
Poetry as read by most people is hardly, if at all,
distinguishable from prose, unless it be for the recurrence of rhymes; and it is correct, I believe, to
say that not a single actor on the English stage
to-day recites blank verse so as to distinguish it
clearly from prose. Edwin Booth was the last,
so far as I know, to preserve a nice obedience to
the rhythmising instinct, while never sacrificing
the sense to it.

The proper reading of verse is thus a cunning
compromise between our rhythmising instinct and
the normal prose pronunciation of the words.
The compromise varies with every reader and
with each reader's differing moods; and for this
reason, if for no other, any attempt to adopt a precise schematisation for verse must fail of general
validity. The old system of macrons and breves
with the accent is probably the best, after all, so

long as we remember that in Greek, and still
more in English, such a system represents only a
rough approximation of the reality. Listen to a
good reader attentively, and for a while you will
be able to beat time to the rhythm of the verse as
accurately as to music; then suddenly, through
some stress of feeling or some desire to avoid
monotony, the rhythm will be loosened to an un-
measured flow of sounds, only to fall again into
the regular singsong. The final impression sug-
gests the rhythm of music, only much freer and
more capricious than a musician could properly
give to his performance. If we may trust a large
number of anecdotes, the great poets, in reading
their own verse, pronounced it with a strong singsong effect, showing that they had in their minds
an ideal rhythm of perfect ratios, from which
every deviation seemed to them an irregularity.
It is probable, too, that the Greeks and Romans
chanted their verse with much more of musical
singsong than seems permissible to our more
sophisticated ears.

ARTHUR SYMONS: THE TWO ILLUSIONS

IT is a saying of Joubert, as subtle as it is true, that the essence of art is to be found in the union of *l'illusion et la sagesse*,—illusion and, to extend the meaning of the French phrase somewhat, dis-illusion; and for one who cares to penetrate into the secret influences of poetry on the human heart, no better guide can be suggested than this brief sentence. But like all such generalisations it is susceptible of a false application in practice as well as a right one, a distinction which has been newly and emphatically attested by the publication of the collected poems of Mr. Arthur Symons. For there is a true illusion without which poetry can-not exist, without which it sinks to the level of unimaginative prose or passes into the thin aridi-ties of metaphysics. In its simplest form this illusion may, perhaps, be seen in the pastoral world of our Elizabethan poets, in the *Lycidas* and *Comus* of Milton best of all; and the skill to lend reality to these idyllic dreams might even seem one of the surest tests of a poet's right to deal with the high illusion of art. *Lycidas* springs from this theme just as much as the youthful

Pastorals of Pope, but what a chasm there lies between them! As the poet's thoughts and aspirations are lifted up beyond the thoughts of common men, so he is able without violating artistic illusion to carry his reader into ideal scenes never beheld on this earth. The noble isolation of Milton's soul schooled him to speak understandingly the ideal language of Arcadia, and something within our souls responds to every word. But in the mouth of a worldling like Pope this language becomes a shallow affectation and conveys no illusion of reality to the reader.

And if you wish to see the power of poetic illusion exemplified in a more general form than the pretty deceptions of Arcadia, turn to any of the greater plays of Shakespeare, to *Hamlet*, which will make you believe for the space of a few hours that human life really revolves about such mystic musings and expresses itself in such rapt language as the mad Dane's, or to *The Tempest*, in which the poet has symbolised his own powers of enchantment in the wizard Prospero. And yet, side by side with this illusion, there must always in the greater poets run a note of disillusion,—a note subdued for the most part so as scarcely to be heard, but rising to the surface now and again with a strange quivering of mingled sadness and joy, of sadness for the fair enchantment it dispels, of joy for the glimpse it affords into something divine and very high. You may hear this note of disillusion many times in Shakespeare, clearest of

all in *The Tempest*, where with a word Prospero
puts an end to his fairy drama in the woods, and
all the insubstantial pageant fades away.

For one acquainted with Oriental literature it is
impossible to reflect on this illusion of art without
recurring to the Hindu doctrine of Mâyâ, who is
supposed to be the creative force of all this wonderful web of appearances that enwrap the spirit in
their mesh and charm the spirit's attention by
their mystery of beauty and seeming benevolence.
To the Oriental, as often to the man of the West
who considers the character of this illusion, Mâyâ
assumes the form of the eternal-feminine unfolding
her allurements before the masculine looker-on.
So in the book of one of the two great philosophies
of India the story of illusion and disillusion is told
in this metaphor of the stage:

> Like as a dancing-girl to sound of lyres
> Delights the king and wakens sweet desires
>   For one brief hour, and having shown her art
> With lingering bow behind the scene retires:
>
> So o'er the Soul alluring Nature vaunts
> Her lyric spell, and all her beauty flaunts;
>   And she, too, in her time withdrawing leaves
> The Watcher to his peace—'t is all she wants.
>
> Now have I seen it all! the Watcher saith,
> And wonders that the pageant lingereth:
>   And, He hath seen me! then the Other cries,
> And wends her way: and this they call the Death.

And when the play is seen, the illusion dispelled,
and the dancing has disappeared, for a while the

watcher waits in quiet, seeming to live the old life, as a potter's wheel revolves a little space after the potter's hand is still; but in reality the desire of this world is ended and in his time he withdraws into the untroubled peace of his nature. It is called Death; it is also called the Awakening. It is a consummation of philosophy not unmixed with joy, though it may seem empty to most Western minds. It is even in another way the consummation of poetry, for ever and anon, as we have seen, the true poet lifts for a moment the very veil of illusion he is weaving and shows us glimpses of what is beyond. And that is well. But suppose, when the play is ended, there is no wisdom of self-knowledge attained, no spiritual joy to take the place of the old lust of the eyes, no royal watcher sitting serenely apart, but only some poor outcast of the street, a brother in life to the painted dancer on the stage—what then?

Now the story of such an illusion and such an awakening is the theme of the poems which Mr. Arthur Symons has recently collected and published in two volumes. In one group of these poems the parallel to the Oriental conception of the dancing-girl is so marked that the author would almost seem to have had the impressing of this moral in his mind when he wrote them. I refer to *The Dance of the Seven Sins*, *The Lover of the Queen of Sheba*, and *The Dance of the Daughters of Herodias*, in each of which the poet

imagines the allurements of the world as dancing
before the eyes of some tempted watcher.

> Is it the petals falling from the rose?
> For in the silence I can hear a sound
> Nearer than my own heart-beat, such a word
> As roses murmur, blown by a great wind.
> I see a pale and windy multitude
> Beaten about the air, as if the smoke
> Of incense kindled into visible life
> Shadowy and invisible presences;
> And, in the cloudy darkness, I can see
> The thin white feet of many women dancing,
> And in their hands . . .

That is the illusion of the world and of the desires of the world, daughters of Herodias dancing
before the grey face of Herod.   And as they dance
they sing—

> "For are not we," they say, "the end of all?
> Why should you look beyond us? If you look
> Into the night, you will find nothing there:
> We also have gazed often at the stars.
> We, we alone among all beautiful things,
> We only are real: for the rest are dreams."

But the watcher grows weary of the long monotony of the scene:

> Have I not seen you as you are
> Always, and have I once admired
> Your beauty?   I am very tired,
> Dancers, I am more tired than you.
> When shall the dance be all danced through?

It is the beginning of wisdom, you say, the cry of
the Hindu watcher, " Lo, I have seen it all!"
and yet—

> Wisdom is weariness to me.
> For wisdom, being attained, but shows
> That all things are but shadows cast
> On running water, swiftly past,
> And as the shadow of the rose
> That withers in the mirror glassed.

And that is the outcome—" Wisdom is weariness!"

> O bondslave, bondslave unto death,
> Might I but hope that death should free
> This self from its eternity!

It was, you see, a false illusion that could lead
only to a false awakening; it is utterly different
from the true illusion such as hovers over the
pastoral world of *Lycidas* and works through the
magic of Prospero, and the awakening from it is
equally different from the disillusion of Shakespeare or of the Hindu philosopher. The true
illusion does not confuse the things of the spirit
with the things of the world. It knows that for
a while the way of the spirit must lie through
this ἄτης λειμῶνα, this meadow-land of calamity,
and its office is by a deliberate effort of the will to
throw the glamour of light and joy and freedom
on the objects by the roadside, so that the spirit
may journey swiftly and pleasantly to its own

upland home. And when its task is completed it
leaves the spirit at rest with itself, without regret
or further craving, filled with the consummation
of peace that springs from experience and self-
knowledge, while the world of the senses remains
in memory only so far as this world shadows the
spirit's own high desires. But the false illusion
is an inner blindness and confusion; it is false because there enters into it no faith in the joy of
things unseen, no knowledge even that such
things exist; it is false because for the voice of the
spirit it hears only the clamorous outcry of a man's
lower personality springing from the desires of
the body and the perceptions of the body, and
is in the end one with what is desired and perceived. At the first this false illusion is sweet,
but soon it is troubled with the bitterness of
satiety; and the awakening from it leaves only
the emptiness of endless regret and self-torment-
ing. The false disillusion is a discovery that the
looker-on who masqueraded as the spirit is merely
a phantom of the body; it is a perception of the
hollowness of the old illusion without the power
of escaping therefrom. The watcher of the Oriental philosophers is one perfectly distinct from
this "self" that cries out to death for deliverance from its own eternity. The disillusion of
the flesh is perhaps the saddest chapter in human
experience.

Now the composition of Mr. Symons's two
volumes is such that we are able to trace the pro-

gress of his poetic mood from the first illusion to
its consummation in a false disillusion; and this
regular gradation we can follow with a precision
which is at least a striking proof of the author's
sincerity. As stated in the prefatory note, these
volumes are made up of selections from five previously published works, viz.: *Days and Nights*,
in 1889; *Silhouettes*, in 1892; *London Nights*, in
1895; *Amoris Victima*, in 1897; and *Images of
Good and Evil*, in 1899; to which is added a
sheaf of new poems, *The Loom of Dreams*. In
one respect the substance of these successive books
is the same; from beginning to end we are in a
land of dreams—dreams always, whether fair or
gloomy, or the haunting remembrance of dreams.
The introductory poem of the first book is a
sonnet that describes the delicious sense of drown-
ing in the gulf of opium, and in like manner the
last poem of all closes with these words in the
mouth of Faustus:

> When Helen lived, men loved, and Helen was:
> I have seen Helen, Helen was a dream,
> I dreamed of something not in Helen's eyes.
> What shall the end of all things be? I wait
> Cruel old age, and kinder death, and sleep.

But if the substance of all these poems is woven
on the same loom of dreams, there is still, as I
have said, a profound change in their colour and
texture as we proceed. Passing over the first
book, from which only a few disconnected poems
9

have been chosen, and these evidently written before the author had arrived at maturity of self-
consciousness, we come to the collection entitled
Silhouettes, which will probably appeal to the
largest circle of readers although they can hardly
be called the strongest specimens of Mr. Symons's
work.   Yet even these poems can never attain to
any wide popularity, nor can they ever have much
weight with practical intelligences that shun the
evanescent world of revery where the real and the
unreal meet and blend together in indistinguishable twilight.   For this atmosphere is one of in-
dulgent brooding; their warp and woof are of the
stuff of dreams woven by a mind that turns from
the actual issues of life as a naked body cowers
from the wind.   The world is seen through a
haze of abstraction, glimmeringly, as a landscape
looms misty and vague through the falling, fluttering veil of the rain.   Indeed it is noteworthy,
how many of the poems descriptive of nature or
of the London streets are drenched with rains and
blown by gusty winds:

> The wind is rising on the sea,
> The windy white foam-dancers leap;
> And the sea moans uneasily,
> And turns to sleep and cannot sleep.
>
> Ridge after rocky ridge uplifts
> Wild hands, and hammers at the land,
> Scatters in liquid dust, and drifts
> To death among the dusty sand.

> On the horizon's nearing line,
> Where the sky rests, a visible wall,
> Grey in the offing, I divine
> The sails that fly before the squall.

And human nature is viewed through a like mist, a mist of tears over laughter, as it may look to one who dreams deliberately while the heart is young and the haunting terror of the awakening seems still something that can be held aloof at his own sweet will. Love is the constant theme, not the great passion of strong men that smites and burns through the world, but the lighter play of emotions that dally and wanton over their own flowering beauty. And these women, to whom the poet's love goes out, girls of the dancing hall and the street, still young and very fair, are only a Western reading of that symbol of nature that dances before the watching soul of the Orient. Their faces steal into the heart with the witchery and insubstantiality of music:

> Across the tides of music, in the night,
> Her magical face,
> A light upon it as the happy light
> Of dreams in some delicious place
> Under the moonlight in the night.

They are not moral and they are not immoral, for they bear no relation to the claims of the soul; they are the figures of a fleeting illusion, a mere blossoming of the flesh yet undefiled:

White girl, your flesh is lilies
Under a frozen moon,
So still is
The rapture of your swoon
Of whiteness, snow or lilies.

Virginal in revealment,
Your bosom's wavering slope,
Concealment,
In fainting heliotrope,
Of whitest white's revealment,

Is like a bed of lilies,
A jealous-guarded row,
Whose will is
Simply chaste dreams: but oh,
The alluring scent of lilies!

So new is the illusion as yet, so fresh this vision of dreams under the spell of white loveliness, that it passes unscathed through the fires of lust:

There with the women, haggard, painted, and old,
One fresh bud in a garland withered and stale,
She, with her innocent voice and her clear eyes, told
Tale after shameless tale.

And ever the witching smile, to her face beguiled,
Paused and broadened, and broke in a ripple of fun,
And the soul of a child looked out of the eyes of a child,
Or ever the tale was done.

The illusion is fair and wonderful; it revels in sweet fragrances and the unforgettable odours of shaken hair; even the artificiality of this desired beauty, its falsities of rouge and pearl-powder, seem but a touch of added spice to make its allurement more pungent. What though he who observes and translates this beauty into rhymes knows that it is only illusion? and what though he who reads and for a while surrenders himself to its sweet intoxication knows it is only illusion? Because the watcher in his real heart penetrates this illusion and knows that it must so soon slip back into the hideous reality, into the painted and haggard ugliness of the flesh that is only flesh and grows old, therefore he feels a greater tenderness for this " frail duration of a flower," and a wistfulness deeper than comes to one who has something of his own spiritual hope to throw over the vanishing loveliness. He is touched by the foreboding of " the little plaintive smile "—

> And those pathetic eyes of hers;
> But all the London footlights know
> The little plaintive smile that stirs
> The shadow in those eyes of hers.

And joined with this tenderness for what must pass away, there is an undercurrent of regret for his own joys that endure so little a space; there is even now, while dreams are the only reality to him, a troublous suspicion rising at intervals that the substance is slipping from his grasp, and this suspicion deepens his regret for the actual past into regret for the evanescent present shadow of things,—

> We are two ghosts that had their chance to live,
> And lost it, she and I.

The poignancy of this tenderness and regret is
something a little different from the sigh that runs
through so much poetry for passing things; it is
the result of a foreboding, half welcome, half
dreaded, that the illusion of this beauty is a
treachery, a snare set by some unseen tempter to
hold a man from his true happiness.   More than
once Mr. Symons compares this illusion to the
smile of Leonardo's Mona Lisa, whose haunted
meaning no man, unless it be perhaps Walter
Pater, has ever interpreted:

> Your smile is like a treachery,
> A treachery adorable;
> So smiles the siren where the sea
> Sings to the unforgetting shell.
>
> .   .   .   .   .
>
> Close lips that keep the secret in,
> Half spoken by the stealthy eyes,
> Is there indeed no word to win,
> No secret, from the vague replies
>
> Of lips and lids that feign to hide
> That which they feign to render up?
> Is there, in Tantalus' dim cup,
> The shadow of water, nought beside?

The shadow of water, indeed, and nothing
more.   There lies the pity of it all.   Suppose the
thirsty watcher of the play suddenly becomes
aware that the pageant is insubstantial shadows,
and that the cup of this world's delight which he
longs to raise to his lips is empty and holds only

the shadow of water—what then? And suppose
that the watcher has no desire in his heart save
this one desire of the world's delight—what then?
That is the terrible disillusion of the flesh, a cruel
mockery of the true awakening; and for the man
on whom it falls — as it must some day fall on
every man of insight, either the false disillusion or
the true awakening—there is nothing left but the
endless rage of endeavour to hold fast an illusion
which no longer deceives, or the sullen apathy
of despair, or the unthinking submission to his
ever coarsening appetites. You will hear the first
note of this coming disillusion in the inevitable
cry of satiety:

> For us the roses are scarce sweet,
> And scarcely swift the flying feet
> Where masque to masque the moments call;
>
> All has been ours that we desired,
> And now we are a little tired
> Of the eternal carnival.

With this word of weariness we pass from the
book of *Silhouettes* to the *London Nights*, published only three years later, and the change is as
marked as it is significant. On the light illusion,
the shimmering web of dreams that spun themselves almost of their own accord, begins to fall the
lengthening shadows of the actual world. The
transient note of satiety becomes more persistent,
and an ever greater effort of the will is required
lest the fluttering curtain of illusion be blown

away and so discover the naked reality which
the watcher dreads to behold. The watcher begins to grow conscious that he is himself a part
of that nature, weary a little and saddened by the
satiety which must continue—for how long?—its
dance of forced gayety.

> My life is like a music-hall,
> Where, in the impotence of rage,
> Chained by enchantment to my stall,
> I see myself upon the stage
> Dance to amuse a music-hall.
>
> .   .   .   .   .
> My very self that turns and trips,
> Painted, pathetically gay,
> An empty song upon the lips
> In make-believe of holiday:
> I, I, this thing that turns and trips!

What we have to observe now is this "impotence of rage" spending itself in the effort to
preserve the fading illusion, or at least to save
some part of that illusion's pleasure. To accom-
plish this all the colours must be heightened and
all the emotions sharpened, though by doing so
the very daintiness and subtlety of impressions
which formed the fascination of the illusion are
stript away and the deprecated end is hastened.

> Ah! no oblivion, for I feel
> Your lips deliriously steal
> Along my neck, and fasten there;
> I feel the perfume of your hair,

> I feel your breast that heaves and dips
> Desiring my desirous lips,
> And that ineffable delight
> When souls turn bodies . . .

Yet even here we are far from the simple passion of the flesh, the passion, for example, of Catullus for his Lesbia, in which there is no talk of souls that turn into bodies but only the natural cry of a man of strong animal appetites and strong unperverted intellect. The morbidness and decadence of Mr. Symons's verse are shown, indeed, in this very hankering after food which to suit a jaded appetite must be unwholesomely spiced with appeals to what is called the soul. He shrinks instinctively from the outright passion of a Catullus, and chooses instead—what?

> " Love is a raging fire,
>   Choose thou content instead;
> Thou, the child of the dust,
>   Choose thou a delicate Lust."
> "Thou hast chosen," I said
>   To the angel of pale desire.

In this same way he cannot pause to find comfort in the homely associations of a love that is less a passion than a quiet haven from the vexations of life. You will find in these volumes nothing corresponding, for example, to the gentle verses of Tibullus counting up the treasures of his love and pastoral content while the morning rain washes on the roof. On the contrary you will

find an artificial passion which requires every
conceivable stimulus to preserve it from passing
into sheer disgust:

> Pallid out of the darkness, adorably white,
> Pale as the spirit of rain, with the night in her hair,
> Renée undulates, shadow-like, under the light,
> Into the outer air.
>
> Mournful, beautiful, calm with that vague unrest,
> Sad with sensitive, vaguely ironical mouth;
> Eyes a-flame with the loveliest, deadliest
> Fire of passionate youth;
>
> Mournful, beautiful, sister of night and rain,
> Elemental, fashioned of tears and fire,
> Ever desiring, ever desired in vain,
> Mother of vain desire.

The morbid unrest that troubles this pallid hot-
house flower is the attraction most of all sought
by the watcher—anything to break the monotony
of the awakening which to him is death.   Even
the sense of shame is welcomed if only it will lend
a little poignancy to this desire that grows chill,
if only it will for a moment continue the illusion
that something in the watcher stands apart from
the play and is above it:

> I too have sought on many a breast
> The ecstasy of an unrest,
> I too have had my dreams, and met
> (Ah me!) how many a Juliet.
>
> .   .   .   .   .

> O lost and wrecked, how long ago,
> Out of the drowning past, I know
> You come to call me, come to claim
> My share of your delicious shame.

And shame at least is ready at hand. Out of this ecstasy of unrest, this morbid curiosity, this terror of satiety, there does spring at last a love that is genuine in its way, a pale amorphous passion, for one whom he calls Bianca. It is a love the telling of which haunts the imagination (so, indeed, it was meant to do) as something not of this world or the other, a thing unclean not with the taint of the untroubled body, but of the body that tortures itself maddeningly to escape from its own insufficiency and masquerade as the soul.

> So the simplicity of flesh
> Held me a moment in its mesh,
> Till that too palled, and I began
> To find that man is mostly man
> In that, his will being sated, he
> Wills ever new variety.
> And then I found you, Bianca! Then
> I found in you, I found again
> That chance or will or fate had brought
> The curiosity I sought.
> Ambiguous child, whose life retires
> Into the pulse of those desires
> Of whose endured possession speaks
> The passionate pallor of your cheeks;
> Child, in whom neither good nor ill
> Can sway your sick and swaying will,
> Only the aching sense of sex

> Wholly controls, and does perplex,
> With dubious drifts scarce understood,
> The shaken currents of your blood;
> It is your ambiguity
> That speaks to me and conquers me.

And the conclusion of the tale is this—"So Bianca satisfies my soul!" It is better to draw the veil of silence over this scene of painfully-won illusion. There are things it were good for a man, even for a decadent poet, not to have written, and these poems to Bianca, with their tortuous effort to find the soul in the ambiguities and unclean curiosities of a swaying will are of them. They are a waste of shame.

The outcome of such an "ecstasy of unrest" is not difficult to foresee, and is the theme of the two following books of the collection, *Amoris Victima* and *Images of Good and Evil*. When the illusion is dispelled, when the ambiguity is found to be merely a deception of the flesh and the curiosity has spent itself in a vain endeavour to discern what does not exist, what can remain but the desolation of emptiness?

> Was not our love fatal to you and me?
> The rapture of a tragic ecstasy
> Between disaster and disaster, given
> A moment's space, to be a hell in heaven?
>
> .   .   .   .
>
> Hearken, I hear a voice, a voice that calls;
> What shall remain for him? sadly it cries:
> Desolate years, eternal memories.

And so the first poems in this book which he calls
Amoris Victima are filled with regrets that at
least come nearer than any others in the collection
to showing the agony of a genuine passion broken
and defeated by some infirmity of the lover's will:

> I am weary of living, and I long to be at rest
> From the sorrowful and immense fatigue of love;
> I have lived and loved with a seeking, passionate zest,
> And weariness and defeat are the end thereof.
>
> I have lived in vain, I have loved in vain, I have lost
> In the game of Fate, and silently I retire;
> I watch the moon rise over the sea, a ghost
> Of burning noontides, pallid with spent desire.

But this sigh of passionate regret for what
seems the loss of a real happiness is but a transient note of honest self-deception. What follows
is the bitter cry of the long struggle, resumed
half-heartedly, between illusion and disillusion.
I do not wish to dwell at length on this struggle,
for it is not entirely pleasant reading, however
great its psychological interest may be. Through
it all runs the memory of the past, but a memory
of shame and not of simple regret:

> O rapture of lost days, all that remains
> Is but this fever aching in my veins.
>
> I do not know you under this disguise:
> I am degraded by my memories.

The thoughts that follow such memories are to
the poet like hideous Harpyes, beaked and taloned,

that gather about him in the darkness of his soul.
And the desires that torture him are the cruel
voice of the flesh from which all illusion has been
torn away, save the persistent denial of relief that
makes of their disillusion a mere mockery of the
true awakening:

> Ah! in those shell-curved, purple eyelids bent
> Towards some most dolorous accomplishment,
> And in the painful patience of the mouth,
> (A sundered fruit that waits, in a great drouth,
> One draught of living water from the skies)
> And in the carnal mystery of the eyes,
> And in the burning pallor of the cheeks;
> Voice of the Flesh! this is the voice that speaks
> In agony of spirit, or in grief
> Because desire dare not desire relief.

In the ocean of these degrading memories,
haunting thoughts, and impuissant desires, the
poor soul (let us call it soul) of the poet is tossed
alternately from the exaltation of terror to the
depths of indifferent despair. He learns at last
that " to have fallen through dreams is to have
touched hell!" As with King Richard dreaming
on Bosworth Field, shadowy images rising from
what has been and clamorous of what is to be,
torment him with a power greater than any
reality of life. The body and substance of this
terror is a vision of emptiness, of the dark void,
that must swallow up the watcher when the
growing disillusion is made complete:

And something, in the old and little voice,
Calls from so farther off than far away,
I tremble, hearing it, lest it draw me forth,
This flickering self, desiring to be gone,
Into the boundless and abrupt abyss
Whereat begins infinity; and there
This flickering self wander eternally
Among the soulless, uncreated winds
Which storm against the barriers of the world.

It is not strange that this outcast self should make
the whole world of God to be a shadow of its own
mood, and that this mood should assume the likeness of insomnia:

Who said the world is but a mood
In the eternal thought of God?
I know it, real though it seem,
The phantom of a haschisch dream
In that insomnia which is God.

There, I think, is the last word to distinguish this
false awakening from the true. From such an
agony of insomnia there can be but one relief, the
repose of utter oblivion and the escape from self in
perfect death. Such in the end and nothing else
is the pleading cry of the disillusioned watcher.

But again this paroxysm of rebellion spends
itself in a little time, and in its place comes the
sigh of lonely indifference and impotence. And I
know not which of these alternating moods should
remain as the last impression of this tragic history. "There are grey hours when I drink of

indifference," he says; and " all things fade Into
the grey of a twilight that covers my soul with its
sky." And again: " The loneliness of the sea
is in my heart, And the wind is not more lonely
than this grey mind." All the wonted rapture
of the world fades into the grey of this impotent
listlessness:

The clamours of spring are the same old delicate noises,
The earth renews its magical youth at a breath,
And the whole world whispers a well-known, secret thing;
And I hear, but the meaning has faded out of the voices;
Something has died in my heart: is it death or sleep?
I know not, but I have forgotten the meaning of spring.

Always while reading these poems, which are
the first full and sincere expression of decadence
in English, with their light and fair illusion passing gradually into the terror of disillusion, I have
heard running through my memory three lines of
old John Ford which contain the very essence of
the right illusion of art (for art, as we have seen,
has its true and necessary illusion of joy as well as
this false illusion of sadness); and involuntarily
these lines would sound out as an echo or counter-
tone to the painfulness of Mr. Symons's lament.
They are like a breath of fresh air let into a murky
chamber:

Since my coming home I 've found
More sweets in one unprofitable dream
Than in my life's whole pilgrimage.

There would be a world of significance in comparing this "coming home" with the wandering of that "flickering self" in the void places of despair.

And yet I would not leave the word despair as the last comment on these poems, which, no matter what their sadness and morbidness may be, stand quite apart from the ordinary versifying of the day. They have, whatever may be said, a great psychological interest for one who is curious to study the currents of modern thought. Mr. Symons impresses us as being absolutely sincere, as being the only genuine and adequate representative in English of that widespread condition which we call decadence. And sincerity in verse is a quality of inestimable value. But more than that: these poems are now and again so instinct with original perception of beauty and so lilted with cadences of sweetness, as to be remarkable in themselves apart from their psychological interest. Toward the end of the second volume, and in the little book of recent poems that close the collection, there forces its way at times, through the turbulent cries of dull desires and stinging regrets, a recurrent note of the first simple delight in nature, — a note which one would gladly accept as prophetic of a new life to arise out of the tragedy of despair. The repose for which the poet sighs in this last poem I would quote, is at least a better and more wholesome thing than the impious oblivion of his earlier craving:

10

REST

The peace of a wandering sky,
Silence, only the cry
Of the crickets, suddenly still,
A bee on the window-sill,
A bird's wing, rushing and soft,
Three flails that tramp in the loft,
Summer murmuring
Some sweet, slumberous thing,
Half asleep; but thou, cease,
Heart, to hunger for peace,
Or, if thou must find rest,
Cease to beat in my breast.

THE EPIC OF IRELAND

In his preface to Lady Gregory's *Cuchulain of Muirthemne*,[1] Mr. Yeats, her good friend, calls it "the best book that has ever come out of Ireland; for," as he says, "the stories it tells are a chief part of Ireland's gift to the imagination of the world." Mr. Yeats is one of the known prophets of the Gaelic revival, and his eulogy may be suspected of the customary national exaggeration; yet to one who comes to Lady Gregory's work from the outside as a lover of beautiful words wherever he may find them, and who brings with him only sufficient sympathy with things Irish to understand their spirit, he trusts, without suffer-

[1] It is an unfortunate drawback to the enjoyment of old Irish literature that the spelling of the proper names gives but the slightest inkling of their pronunciation. The pronunciation commonly adopted is a middle form between the oldest variety, no doubt indicated by the ancient spelling, and the modern variety which, for many of the names, is wanting altogether. Thus the name of the king is spelled Conchubar and was probably pronounced, originally, something like Kón-chovar. The middle form employed in reading the romances is Kŏn-a-chur, while the modern form is Conor. I give a table of the pronunciation of the names occurring in this arti-

ing a perversion of judgment, this praise will sound, not too enthusiastic, but too narrow. He would prefer to hear simply that the *Cuchulain* is one of the great books of the world,—a greater book than many are likely to comprehend until its themes have been caught up and adopted into the body of English literature. I know well enough that the public of the present day is prone to accept the ephemeral clever books and to ignore the true books, and yet I have been surprised to see how little the press in America has had to say of these stories, and how little, comparatively, they have been read,—I say " in America," for I believe that in England they have excited rather more comment. Even if the prosaic Saxon is absorbed in reading the latest novel and the latest treatise on economics, one might suppose that every educated wanderer from Erin would be quick to welcome these superb legends of his old

cle, premising that the vowels have the Italian sound: a as in father, e as in great, i as in machine, o as in note or not, u as in rule or full; ch is almost like k.

Cuchulain of Muirthemne (Ku-chŭ-lin of Mŭr-hĕv-na)
Tain Bo Cuailgne (táun bo chŭln-ya)

Ailell (ăl-yel)   Deirdre (dĕr-dra)
Emer (ĕm-ir)   Levarcham (lă-var-cham)
Conchubar (Kŏn-a-chur)   Maeve (mēv)
Gae Bulg (gē-bulg)   Scathach (skă-ha)
Cathbad (kăf-fa)   Usnach (ŭs-na)
Naoise (nĭ-sha)   Cruachan (krŭ-a-chan)
Ferdiad (fer-dĭ-a)   Sidhe (shĭ).
Findabair (finn-a-var)

home, but there is no sign that such is the case.
I fear it is even necessary to explain somewhat
explicitly who this forgotten Cuchulain was, "this
name to be put in songs," and what these epic
tales of Ireland are.

Though the language Lady Gregory employs
is the quaint vernacular English of modern Ireland, the substance of her book goes back to the
heroic days of the land,— to the seventh and
eighth centuries of our era when Ireland, partly
on account of her isolation from the tumultuous
changes of the continent, blossomed out, just before the terrible coming of the Norsemen, into a
civilisation of rare and passionate beauty.   This
island of the far western seas was in those years
the sacred repository of the learning saved from
the classic past, and boasted to be the teacher of
Europe.   But besides this borrowed culture of
Rome, she possessed a native art of a most peculiar sort.   It was a trait of the Celtic people,
and perhaps to a special degree of that Gaelic
branch of the race which inhabited Ireland, to
honour the poet as the world has hardly elsewhere
seen him honoured.   The bards and fillas (or
higher poets) formed regular schools with an
ollav (or chief poet) at their head.   Their education lasted from seven to twelve years or even
longer, and when complete included the knowledge of more than three hundred and fifty different metres.   As for poetical substance, the ollav
was supposed to have at his command more than

two hundred and fifty prime stories for recitation
and one hundred secondary ones. So numerous
were these bardic reciters that Keating, the historian of the seventeenth century, reckoned their
number at one third of the men of the free clans,
and so formidable was their power that their satire
was said to blast its victim and raise blisters on
his face.

Out of this enormous activity two principal
cycles of song and romance shaped themselves in
the heroic age of Ireland, deriving their substance
in large part from the annals of the great families,
but including, also, confused memories of an
ancient mythology. One of these, the cycle of
Finn and Ossian and Oscar, was long ago vulgarised by the travesties of James Macpherson; the
other, the Cuchulain saga of Ulster, though almost forgotten until recent years, is far the more
important, both for the sweetness and nobility of
the actual stories and for their capability of large
development. The pivot of the whole series, so
to speak, is the famous *Tain Bo Cuailgne* or *Cattle
Raid of Coolney*, which relates how Ailell and
Maeve, king and queen of Connaught, made a
great hosting and drove back with them a magic
brown bull of Ulster. That would seem to lend
itself to a border ballad rather than to the forma-
tion of a true epic; and, indeed, it must not be
supposed that this saga of Ireland possesses the
stately grandeur or the achieved harmony we
connect with the narratives of Greece; it is, at

the best, epic material awaiting the accomplisher. Nevertheless, the deeds of Cuchulain, who, single-handed, opposed the men of Connaught, and above all engaged in tremendous battle with his friend Ferdiad, rise clear out of the regions of mere balladry and, in my opinion, far above the sagas of Germany and Iceland. About this central event are grouped a circle of tales more or less closely connected, and dealing directly or indirectly with the fortunes of Cuchulain and Conchubar, who is related to Cuchulain as Agamemnon was to Achilles. The most beautiful of these subsidiary tales,—so beautiful that one may not hesitate to rank it among the few great stories of tradition,—is the ever memorable *Fate of the Sons of Usnach*, with its fateful heroine, Deirdre,—Deirdre, named of sorrow, " comely beyond comparison of all the women of the world."

The manuscripts in which these tales have been preserved are numerous and date from the eleventh century, when the so-called *Book of the Dun Cow* was transcribed, down to comparatively recent times. Many of the stories had already appeared in excellent literal translations, but it remained for Lady Gregory to make of them an ordered piece of literature. By selecting the tales most closely related and arranging them in proper sequence, she has produced what may be called roughly the Epic of Ireland. To be sure, the same task had already been done—and well done in a way—by Miss Eleanor Hull, but Miss Hull's

work lacks that last creative touch needed to
transfuse the various materials into one homo-
geneous body. This, Lady Gregory, by omit-
ting a little here and there, and by piecing
together from the manifold forms in which the
tales are handed down, has actually accomplished.
There have not been wanting critics, who com-
plain that in this process of moulding Lady Gregory has smoothed away the wild, romantic spirit
that gave the legends their piquancy and value. I
confess that, after a pretty careful comparison of
Lady Gregory's versions with those given in
Miss Hull's volume and elsewhere, I entirely fail
to see the force of this criticism. Almost invari-
ably—I cannot quite say always—her omissions
take away what is puerile or unconvincingly grotesque or extraneous. They can be called a loss,
it seems to me, only by the pedant or the Irish
enthusiast. Again, the additions which she has
imported from manuscripts not used by Miss Hull
or Mr. Whitley Stokes sometimes increase the interest of a story amazingly. As an instance of
such an addition, I would cite this exquisite piece
of romance, which relates how Deirdre was first
brought to the notice of men. Cathbad, the
Druid, had come to the house just after the birth
of Deirdre and had taken the child in his arms
and foretold the evil that was to fall upon men
through her loveliness. And this is what he said:

" Let Deirdre be her name; harm will come through
her. . . .

" In your fate, O beautiful child, are wounds, and ill-doings, and shedding of blood.

" You will have a little grave apart to yourself ; you will be a tale of wonder for ever, Deirdre."

So the young child is given to Lavarcham, her foster-mother, to be brought up in a lonely place, among the hills, where the eye of man shall never light on her fatal dower of beauty.   But here, as always in the realm of story, the radiant gem cannot be concealed:

Lavarcham, that had charge of her, used to be giving Deirdre every knowledge and skill that she had herself. There was not a blade of grass growing from root, or a bird singing in the wood, or a star shining from heaven, but Deirdre had the name of it.   But there was one thing she would not have her know, she would not let her have friendship with any living person of the rest of the world outside their own house.

But one dark night of winter, with black clouds over-head, a hunter came walking the hills, and it so hap-pened that he missed the track of the hunt, and lost his way and his comrades.

And a heaviness came upon him, and he lay down on the side of the green hillock by Deirdre's house.   He was weak with hunger and going, and perished with cold, and a deep sleep came upon him.   While he was lying there a dream came to the hunter, and he thought that he was near the warmth of a house of the Sidhe, [or fairy folk who dwell in the hills,] and the Sidhe in-side making music, and he called out in his dream, " If there is any one inside, let them bring me in, in the name of the Sun and the Moon."   Deirdre heard the voice, and she said to Lavarcham, "Mother, mother,

what is that?" But Lavarcham said, "It is nothing
that matters; it is the birds of the air gone astray, and
trying to find one another. But let them go back to the
branches of the wood." Another troubled dream came
on the hunter, and he cried out a second time. "What
is that?" asked Deirdre again. "It is nothing that matters," said Lavarcham. "The birds of the air are looking for one another; let them go past to the branches of
the wood." Then a third dream came to the hunter,
and he cried out a third time, if there was any one in
the hill to let him in for the sake of the Elements, for
he was perished with cold and overcome with hunger.
"Oh! what is that, Lavarcham?" said Deirdre. "There
is nothing there for you to see, my child, but only the
birds of the air, and they lost to one another, but let
them go past us to the branches of the wood. There is
no place or shelter for them here to-night." "Oh,
mother," said Deirdre, "the bird asked to come in for
the sake of the Sun and the Moon, and it is what you
yourself told me, that anything that is asked like that,
it is right for us to give it. If you will not let in the
bird that is perished with cold and overcome with
hunger, I myself will let it in." So Deirdre rose up
and drew the bolt from the leaf of the door, and let in
the hunter.

This is not only exquisite in itself,—purer,
sweeter romance will not easily be found though
many ancient books be searched,—but it is necessary to the *éthos* of the events, as an Aristotelian
would say, and the omission of it in Miss Hull's
version leaves the story maimed of its fairest
member. It shows very well, moreover, the
quaint language Lady Gregory has chosen for her
translation,—the spoken dialect of her beloved

Ireland, very simple and colloquial yet touched with I know not what glamour of pathos and lyric passion in accord with the old-world romance of the legends. To follow Deirdre through the adventures of her tragic life; to tell how she is wooed by Conchubar, the King of Ulster; how she avoids the royal suitor and bestows her coveted love upon Naoise, the son of Usnach; how she flees with Naoise and his two brothers to Scotland; how they are lured back to Ireland; how Deirdre on the way prophesies of the evils to come; how the three sons of Usnach are treacherously slain; and how Deirdre by the waves of the sea gives up her young life that she may cheat the cruel king of so much loveliness and that she may not be parted from the three dear sons of Usnach, —all this would be to transgress the limits of an essay; and is it not written out fairly in the book ? I cannot read this story of Deirdre, with her dower of fatal beauty and her wild, uncredited prophesyings of woe, without recalling the two heroines of Greece, Helen and Cassandra, whose characters she seems to bear strangely blended together; and I think if one does not set her lamentations among the noblest lyric poems of the world, he may be certain, as Mr. Yeats says, that the wine-press of the poets has been trodden for him in vain.

But Deirdre is not the only notable heroine in these tales. There is Emer of the yellow hair, of the fair form, whom Cuchulain took to wife after the long courting and after the high training in

heroism under Scathach, the mystic woman of
Scotland, there where he met Ferdiad his companion in arms. Emer, too, like Deirdre, knew
the toils of fate, and her jealousy of Fand, the
woman from beyond the waves of the great sea, is
one of the memorable passions of the book. And,
like Deirdre, she, too, in the end sang a marvellous lamentation over the body of her fallen lord.
There is Maeve, the bloodthirsty queen of Connaught, who spurred on her people and knew no
rest till she got for herself the magic bull of
Cuailgne. And there is her daughter Findabair,
of the fair eyebrows,—she whose love was promised by Maeve to the many champions who went
out to slay Cuchulain, and last of all to Ferdiad
to hearten him in the sad combat. But always
Findabair cherished in her breast the passion she
had felt for one dear, murdered suitor who was
dear also to the Sidhe; and when she heard how
her love had been promised to one champion after
another and had caused their death, then, as the
story relates, '' her heart broke with the shame
and the pity and she fell dead, and they buried
her.''

It must not be supposed, however, that these
heroines, attractive and human as they are, over-
shadow the warriors and princes and prophetic
Druids who move through these scenes of adventure, or that the clamour and pathos of woman's
love drown out the sound of battle-cry and the
glory of mighty deeds. Still the epic valour of

men overrides all, the κλέα ανδρῶν, as it should in great stories. Our interest here, as Wordsworth felt on hearing the song of the Gaelic lass, is still

> For old, unhappy, far-off things,
> And battles long ago.

I am tempted in this connection to quote a little from the famous duel of Cuchulain and Ferdiad, if only to balance the softer passages of Deirdre's solitude. It is told in *The Cattle Raid of Coolney*. The clans of Ailell and Maeve had marched into Ulster, and, owing to a strange disease that held the other men of Ulster in bondage, Cuchulain alone was free to oppose the advancing host. This he does so effectually that day after day a selected champion of Connaught falls at his hands. At last, with the lure of Findabair's love, Maeve rouses Ferdiad, the old companion of Cuchulain in Scotland, to go out against the dreaded hero. Thereupon follows the battle of four days, with its contest of alternating pity and wrath, and its mingling of

> All passions of a fight unmatched till then
> On warfields of the immemorial world.

And this is how their fighting and resting on the first day is told:

So they began with their casting weapons, and they took their protecting shields, and their round-handled spears, and their little quill spears, and their ivory-hilted knives, and their ivory-hafted spears, eight of each of them they had, and these were flying from them and to them like bees on the wing on a fine summer day; there was no cast that did not hit, and each one went on shooting at the other with those weapons from the twilight of the early morning to the full midday, until all their weapons were blunted against the faces and the bosses of the shields. And as good as the throwing was, the defence was so good that neither of them drew blood from the other through that time.

"Let us leave these weapons now, Cuchulain," said Ferdiad, "for it is not by the like of them our fight will be settled." "Let us leave them, indeed, if the time be come," said Cuchulain.

They stopped then, and threw their darts into the hands of their chariot-drivers. "What weapons shall we use now, Cuchulain?" said Ferdiad. "The choice of weapons is yours till night," said Cuchulain. "Let us, then," said Ferdiad, "take to our straight spears, with the flaxen strings in them." "Let us now, indeed," said Cuchulain. And then they took two stout shields, and they took to their spears.

Each of them went on throwing at the other with the spears from the middle of midday until the fall of the evening. And good as the defence was, yet the throwing was so good that each of them wounded the other in that time.

"Let us leave this now," said Ferdiad. "Let us leave it, indeed, if the time has come," said Cuchulain.

So they left off, and they threw their spears away from them into the hands of their chariot-drivers. Each of them came to the other then, and each put his hands round the neck of the other, and gave him three kisses. Their horses were in the one enclosure that night, and their chariot-drivers at the one fire; and their chariot-drivers spread beds of green rushes for them, with wounded men's pillows on them.

So the battle continued for three days, but on the fourth day, when the choice of weapons came a second time to Cuchulain, he chose the Gae Bulg, a mystical spear that no man could withstand, and on that day Ferdiad knew that he was to die. The lament of the victor over his fallen friend is one of the unforgettable lyrics of the book. And " this thing will hang over me for ever," he cried in the end. " Yesterday he was larger than a mountain; to-day there is nothing of him but a shadow."

I am aware that passages of this kind, when torn from their context, convey very feebly the original impression of the scene. Indeed, the excellence of these stories is not of the ballad sort that can be transferred to a page, but has the epic effect that comes from the accumulation or gradual development of interest. It depends on plot, in the Aristotelian sense of the word, on events, that is, so disposed as to bring out heroic traits of character and to lead up to some supreme emotion. Now in so far as the Irish legends possess these qualities they merely conform to the model of the great story wherever and in whatever language it may be found. But they do possess, also, certain subsidiary qualities which quite distinguish them from other literatures, and which lend them a peculiar interest apart from plot and characterisation and apart from the universal elements of humour and pathos and passion and sublimity.

And here I cannot help regretting that this

body of Gaelic romance, altogether the finest
product of the Celtic genius, was unknown to
Renan and to Matthew Arnold when they wrote
their respective essays. I can imagine how sub-
tilely they would have drawn out these subsidiary
qualities and set forth the distinctive spirit of the
Gael.   Renan would not have dwelt so strongly
on *isolation* as the master trait of Celtic character:
Matthew Arnold would not, I think, have laid
quite the same emphasis on *sentiment*; he would,
perhaps, have laid even greater stress on the
word *magic*, on the Celtic " gift of rendering with
wonderful felicity the magical charm of nature."
Magic is, indeed, as he reiterates in his way, just
the word for it, but he would have given to the
term a meaning fraught with far more of human
emotion and less of fairy enchantment.   He drew
his inferences from the *Mabinogion*,—tales of the
Cymri, another branch of the Celtic race, which
are to the Gaelic epos as a child's book is to a
man's.   He would have found in the prose and
verse of the Irish Gael the same delicacy and
charm of magical description as in the Cymric
tales, but he would have caught, also, a deeper
note of magic power vibrant with passionate
possibilities.

There is an ancient poem which tradition
holds to have been uttered by Amergin, the
son of Milesius, when, at the coming of the
wanderers, he, first of the Gaels, set foot on Irish
soil:

> I am the wind which blows o'er the sea;
> I am the wave of the deep;
> I am the bull of seven battles;
> I am the eagle on the rock;
> I am a tear of the sun;
> I am the fairest of plants;
> I am a boar for courage;
> I am a salmon in the water;
> I am a lake in the plain;
> I am the word of knowledge.

This is not an expression of pantheism, as some have interpreted it, but of that kinship with the powers of nature, which never left the Gael and which rises at times to a sense of magical identification. And always it is the medium of his emotion. So when Cuchulain has fought the lamentable battle with his son, who is unknown to him at first and is discovered only in death, he breaks out into a cry of anguish that is like an echo of the song of the first Gael:

> "I am the father that killed his own son, the fine green branch; there is no hand or shelter to help me.
> "*I am a raven that has no home; I am a boat going from wave to wave; I am a ship that has lost its rudder; I am the apple left on the tree;* it is little I thought of falling from it; grief and sorrow will be with me from this time."

Nearness to nature was the very birthright of the Gael. No warrior of the land was without this sympathy, not even the great Finn, type of all warriors in later times. Dr. Sigerson has

11

translated a haunting song in which Ossian, the
son of Finn, relates to St. Patrick his father's
love of bird and deer and sighing waters:

> The tuneful tumult of that bird,
> The belling deer on ferny steep;
> This welcome in the dawn he heard,
> These soothed at eve his sleep.
>
> Dear to him the wind-loved heath,
> The whirr of wings, the rustling brake;
> Dear the murmuring glens beneath,
> And sob of Droma's lake.

And as man is bound thus closely to Nature, so
she in turn often assumes a human likeness that
comes out in little touches of metaphor and personification. When, for example, one of the
Ulster men went out to explore, his way of return
lay across a river. " But he gave a false leap,"
the story says, "just where the water was deepest,
and a wave laughed over him, and he died."

But these are lesser things. A more striking
outcome of this magical identification (which
passes far beyond the charm found by Matthew
Arnold in the *Mabinogion*) is seen in what may
be called the prophetic or foreboding sympathy of
nature. By some mystic bond the waves of river
and lake, the wide-flowing winds, the clouds, and
the living creatures that grow upon the earth are
all prescient of the fate of the Gael and give signs
of what is to befall him, so that he walks among
them as through a world of riddling adumbra-

tions. Thus before the great battle, when the
sick men of Ulster arouse themselves to meet the
hosting of Connaught, Mac Roth, the herald, goes
out to learn tidings of them for Ailell and Maeve,
" and he had not long to wait before he heard a
noise that was like the falling of the sky, or the
breaking in of the sea over the land, or the falling
of trees on one another in a great storm." And
this is the report he brings back to the king and
queen: " I thought I saw a grey mist far away
across the plain, and then I saw something like
falling snow, and then through the mist I saw
something shining like sparks from a fire, or like
the stars on a very frosty night." It is not necessary to remark how skilfully real appearances are
here mingled with metaphor and magic foreboding;
for the cloud was the dust that went up from the
marching men of Ulster, and the flakes of snow
were the foam flakes from their champing horses,
and the stars were their angry eyes gleaming
under their helmets. Other passages, more prophetic and less clearly metaphorical than this,
might be quoted, but none, perhaps, more characteristic of the Gaelic manner. Again, this mystic
adumbration takes the form of a dream, as when
the High King Conaire foresees his doom. And
it is what he said: " I had a dream in my sleep a
while ago, of the howling of my dog Oscar, of
wounded men, of a wind of terror, of keening that
overcame laughter." Or again, the warning
passes still further beyond the scope of ordinary

phenomena and becomes a waking vision of the day that appears with symbolic form. In this manner, before his death, Cuchulain goes forth with Cathbad, the Druid, and, coming to a ford, beholds " a young girl, thin and white-skinned and having yellow hair, washing and ever washing, and wringing out clothing that was stained crimson red, and she crying and keening all the time."

Not unrelated to this kind of visionary symbolism is another device of the Irish story-tellers which forms one of the commonest features of their art. It is a trick that Homer used to describe the army of Greece, and that Sir Walter Scott has made familiar to modern readers in the scene where Rebecca looks out from the tower and relates to Ivanhoe the progress of the siege. No more certain means is known to lend vividness and human interest to a narrative, and our *raconteurs* have not been slow to take profit therefrom. Now this rhetorical device was long ago employed by the Gaelic poets,— employed so frequently and with such mingling of magic vision that it is on the whole the most striking peculiarity of their art. Not unlike the simple manner of Sir Walter is the account of the great battle given by his chariot driver to Cuchulain, while the warrior lies wounded after his duel with Ferdiad; only hardly in Sir Walter will you find any expression of passionate regret like the cry of Cuchulain, " My grief ! I not to be able to go among them!'' More symbolic and Gaelic in spirit is the scene before the raid, when the heroes of Ulster come to Cruachan, the stronghold of Maeve, that the queen may decide which of them deserves the title of champion. The sound of their furious driving reaches the listeners in the castle, and then it was that ''Findabair of the Fair Eyebrows, daughter of Ailell and Maeve, went up, for she had a bird's sight, to her sunny parlour over the great door of the fort, to tell them what was coming.'' One after another she describes the various heroes in the chariots with their host of followers. At last she beholds Cuchulain, and she cries out:

" I see in the chariot a dark sad man, comeliest of the men of Ireland. A plaited crimson tunic about him, fastened at the breast with a brooch of inlaid gold; a long-sleeved linen cloak on him with a white hood embroidered with flame-red gold. His eyebrows as black as the blackness of a spit, seven lights in his eyes, seven colours about his head, love and fire in his look. Across his knees there lies a gold-hilted sword, there is a blood-red spear ready to his hand, a sharp-tempered blade with a shaft of wood. Over his shoulders a crimson shield with a rim of silver, overlaid with shapes of beasts in gold."

There is more here than mere description, or than the prevailing love of these tellers for radiant many-blended colours; the blood-red spear is ready to the hero's hand, and we feel the onrushing of

some tremendous event.   And Maeve in her mind
knows the meaning of the vision and interprets
it: " Like the sound of an angry sea, like a great
moving wave, with the madness of a wild beast
that is vexed, he leaps through his enemies in the
crash of battle; they hear their death in his shout.
He heaps deed upon deed, head upon head; his
is a name to be put in song."

A name to be put in song!   I come in truth to
what lies nearest my heart in this attempt to
awaken interest in a book of ancient legends.   It
is well that scholars should make for us a literal,
studiously exact translation of these tales, like,
for example, Miss Winifred Farraday's *Cattle
Raid of Cuailgne*, lately published in the Grimm
Library; it is well, still better in my judgment,
that Lady Gregory has gathered them together
and wrought them into something approaching
epic unity; best of all will it be when these inspiring themes have been absorbed into the body
of English literature, and have given us, as I
doubt not they will give, great poems that are
both English and modern, yet are pervaded with
that fructifying spirit of true romance which it
has been the one high office of the Celtic peoples
to bestow upon the world.   When I see the eager
and vain search for substance in nearly all our living poets, their mere schoolgirl's delight in pretty
nature embroidered in pretty words, or even Kipling's melodious Jingoism, I am amazed that some
one of them does not fall upon this treasure-house

of unrifled inspiration to write for us a new epic,
—a truer epic than Tennyson's *Idyls of the King*,
for he would not be seduced into the sentimentalism that clings to so much of the Arthurian tradition.   Here at his asking is a theme to which
he might devote all his genius, a labour for which
he might strive, like Milton, to make of himself
first of all a true poem, or school himself in manifold learning like the ollav of ancient days.

I know that Cuchulain and his achievements
have exercised many recent poets of Ireland, but
the right singer has not yet arisen.   Ferguson
was brave and manly, but lacked the flower of art;
Aubrey de Vere was cultured and sensitive, but
wanted the informing spirit of originality, so that
his blank verse is Miltonic and Tennysonian by
turns, a thing of shreds and patches.   There is,
to be sure, the younger candidates of the Gaelic
revival, but somehow too much of their work
shows the shimmering hues of decadence rather
than the strong colours of life.   It is a paradox,
and yet I believe it is true, that if ever these
themes are worked over and moulded into the
universal form of modern art, it will be by Saxon
hands and not by Celtic.   Some fatal weakness
would seem to adhere to this gifted race of the
Celts, some incapacity that comes on them, as the
sickness came on the men of Ulster when the need
was most urgent, and prevents them from inherit-
ing the perfect product of their own imagination.
The hated Saxon shall lay hold of their spiritual

heritage as he has taken possession of their land, and no clamorous outcry of patriotic scholars and of Gaelic leagues shall inhibit him. In the same way it was the Celt who originated the legend of King Arthur and his Court, the fairest creation of the Middle Ages, but it remained for the French- man to take up the subject and shape it and rationalise it until it grew to be the fountain-head of European literature. There is a tradition still held among the Gaels that Finn and his mighty comrades are not dead but sleeping, and that one day they shall arouse themselves and restore the Gael to his national inheritance, just as the Welsh look for the coming of King Arthur. It is related that a lonely wanderer in the hills chanced upon their resting-place and saw there a horn with the command graven on it that it should be blown three times. Once he blew, and the sleepers, men and dogs, stirred in their slumber. A second time he blew, and the warriors rose on their elbows and gazed at him expectantly. But his nerve failed him then and he fled in terror from the ghostly spectacle,—with the cry of the prisoners ringing in his ears, "A thousand curses on you; you have left us worse than you found us!" And they are still sleeping, waiting for the bold Saxon who shall come and shall wind the magic horn the third time and not be afraid. A dreamer to the end the Celt remains, but the waking power of the controlling poet for ever eludes him:

Alone among his kind he stands alone,
  Torn by the passions of his own sad heart;
Stoned by continual wreckage of his dreams,
  He in the crowd for ever is apart.

And besides this inefficiency of the dreamer,
there is in the leaders of the so-called Gaelic revival, a spirit which militates against the production of pure art.   One feels constantly that these
poets and romancers are too little concerned with
literature for its own sweet sake, and too much
bent, as Spenser wrote long ago, who knew the
Irish people so well, on " the hurt of the English
and the maintenance of their owne lewd libertie."
That is a phrase—" their owne lewd libertie"
—which expresses admirably the lack of inner restraint, of the final shaping force, that made of
these Cuchulain tales, even in the heroic days
when Ireland was capable of great things, a collection of epic fragments marvellously shot
through with lyric beauty, instead of a completed
work of art such as Greece and Rome were able to
create.   It is as if the poet, with all his fire and
insight,—poet truly though he may have spoken
in prose,—never fully understood the material he
was working in, and so failed at the last to develop what came to him as an initial inspiration.
And this failure shows itself in sins both of com-
mission and omission.

There is, first of all, a vein of childishness
which crops up too often just when the tone

should be most serious and tragic. It is characteristic that in the original quarrel of Ailell and
Maeve, on which the whole central story of the
raid hinges, there should be a bit of puerile talk
about a white-horned bull who had left Maeve's
herd for Ailell's because he did not think it was
fitting to be under the rule of a woman. Or, to
mention a single other example, in the very midst
of the tremendous feats of Cuchulain the reader
is suddenly shocked out of his tragic sympathy by
hearing that the champion smeared blackberries
on his face to give himself the appearance of a
beard. Not unlike this childishness is the recurring note of exaggeration and grotesque supernaturalism; it is the magic of the Celt run riot.
To compare these stories with the *Iliad*,—and not
seldom the comparison is perfectly legitimate,—
the effect is the same as if the battle of the gods
and the incredible events at the Scamander were
broken up and scattered indiscriminately throughout the Trojan war. These are sins of commis-
sion which only mean in the end that the
Cuchulain saga, with all its incomparable poetry,
is in its present form mediæval and not classic
and universal.

And there are faults of omission which tend to
the same result, and which show that the poet,
despite his noble inspiration, was never quite
master of his theme. They are errors of construction chiefly, a failure to perceive clearly the great
moments of a story and to prepare the mind of the

reader for them in advance.   Thus there is a certain resemblance between Cuchulain's use of the magic Gae Bulg on the last day of the duel with Ferdiad and the arming of Achilles for his supreme encounter with Hector; but mark the difference.   No adequate preparation is made in the Irish tale for this event; the very name of the weapon is almost a surprise to the reader and its form and nature are left altogether obscure, whereas a long episode in the *Iliad* is devoted to the making of Achilles's shield.[1]   Again, a poet quite sure of his art would have developed the friendship of Cuchulain and Ferdiad early in the narrative and thus have given some foreboding of the tragic climax.   A more luminous illustration may be found in a comparison of the prophetic fate of the two heroes, Cuchulain and Achilles.   Both are aware that life is short for them, that early death is the price they must pay for glory among men and fame eternal in song. When Cuchulain is a boy at play in the fields he hears Cathbad, the Druid, declare that if any young man should take arms on that day his name would be greater than any other name in Ireland, but his span of life would be brief.   And " it is little I would care," said Cuchulain, " if

[1] It is hardly necessary to say that I am aware of the criticism which makes this episode a late addition to the poem.   I speak of the *Iliad* as it stands, with all its inconsistencies, still the most perfectly constructed poem devised by man or men.

my life were to last one day and one night only,
so long as my name and the story of what I have
done would live after me.'' That is well, but
somehow it is a little lacking in emotional content, and the foreboding of the hero's death is
quite forgotten in the story that follows.   Instinctively we recall the scene of the Greek hero,
sitting in solitude and brooding over his destiny:

But Achilles sat far apart from his companions, weeping, on the shore of the grey sea, looking out over the
illimitable ocean; and much he besought his dear mother
with outstretched hands: " Mother, since thou hast
born me for a brief and little life, at least Zeus, the
Thunderer on high Olympus, should have bestowed
honour upon me."

And always throughout the vicissitudes of the
Iliad we remember what destiny hovers over the
young warrior.   In the different employment of
this similar material one feels the distinction between great poetry in its embryonic state and
poetry fully wrought out and achieved.

The same inefficiency penetrates even deeper
into the Irish genius.   In his study of *The Celtic
Doctrine of Rebirth*, Mr. Alfred Nutt has, with no
little acumen, set forth the likeness of the early
mythological age of Ireland to the period in
Greece when the Dionysiac cult was developed.
He finds in the Sidhe, or fairy folk of the Gael,
the same powers of life and increase which were
personified in the Hellenic god of death and

rebirth, of wine and frenzied ecstasy. It is significant that in Ireland these powers became a
tricky race whose acts were inwrought with the
longing of the people for a fair, shadowy other-
world, a Tirnanog or land of the always young, a
heaven of dreams, very beautiful and winsome,
appearing here and there in vision to the lonely
wanderer and inspiring his lyric joys, but without
moral intent or serious influence; whereas from
Dionysus and the mystery of his passion sprang,
in Greece, the greatest and most profoundly moral
drama the world has ever seen. Yet—and this,
too, it is fair to say—Dionysus and the tragedy
of Greece have passed away, while the simple
peasant of Ireland still beholds glimpses of the
happy Sidhe, and still hears the voices luring him
away to some Land of Youth that lies beyond the
hills or over the western sea. I cannot but think
that the band of disciples who are attempting to
re-create to-day a literature of Ireland in the Irish
tongue are seduced by the same impalpable visions
that have hovered about their pathetic land from
the beginning. In the day of his strength the
Gael prepared for the world a body of inspiration,
whose haunting but imperfect beauty I have tried
to set forth; now the inheritance lies open to all
people and awaits the cunning hand of the
stranger who shall make it his own.

Yet the honour shall, nevertheless, in a way be
Ireland's. One poet the new movement has produced, Irish in birth but Saxon and Greek in

training,—Lionel Johnson,—whose early death is
still lamented.   The restrained power of his ode
on the sorrows of Ireland might seem to justify
the hopes of the most extravagant patriots, were
it not that the form and manner of his writing
show more of the Saxon than of the Gael:

> And yet great spirits ride thy winds: thy ways
> Are haunted and enchaunted evermore.
> Thy children hear the voices of old days
> In music of the sea upon thy shore,
> In falling of the waters from thine hills,
>   In whispers of thy trees:
> A glory from the things eternal fills
> Their eyes, and at high noon thy people sees
> Visions, and wonderful is all the air.
>   So upon earth they share
> Eternity: they learn it at thy knees.

P. S.— Since the writing of this essay Lady Gregory
has completed her survey of the Irish Sagas by publishing her *Gods and Fighting Men*, in which she has
brought together into a single volume the Fenian tales
and the legends concerned with the settling of Ireland
and with the races of gods. It must be admitted that,
from no fault of the translator's, the interest of these
later tales is decidedly inferior to that of the earlier.
There is nothing like the same unity of effect as in
the Cuchulain saga, and none of the individual stories in
any way approaches the beauty and sublimity of *The
Fate of the Sons of Usnach*. The majority of the tales
are about the Fenians, and it is perfectly evident that,
as Dr. Hyde maintains, they are bits of mere folklore

which have been popular in the mouths of the un-
educated Irish for many hundreds of years; indeed, not
a few of them can be heard in peasant homes to-day.
They are thus peculiarly exposed to that looseness of
conception, that incoherence and failure to grip the
subject, which Matthew Arnold long ago pointed out
as the essential weakness of the Celtic genius. The
Cuchulain tales, on the contrary, seem never to have
enjoyed the same common popularity. They were apparently the property of the great families, and were
told for the benefit of nobles in the banquet hall, much
after the fashion of the Homeric chants. As a consequence they have received more of the discipline of
the shaping imagination, and their emotional content
has been deepened and concentrated. The Fenian saga
is composed for the most part of curious fairy tales,
wherein the law of cause and effect is entirely forgotten
and the reader wanders in a land of childish surprises;
the Cucnulain is an embryonic epic shot through with
the radiant colours of the " magic " of the Celt.

I do not mean to imply by this that the later tales are
without a beauty of their own, but that this beauty is of
a more scattered and unintentional nature. Finn was the
captain of a band of Janissaries (if we may accept the
historic explanation of the legends), who were called
the Fenians (Fianna), and who gradually usurped more
and more power until under Cormac, High King of
Ireland, they were crushed in a great battle and put
down. The stories about these banded soldiers are of
endless battles and brawls and hunting adventures,
wherein demons and fairy folk and marvellous beasts
and vanishing scenes play a principal part.

It is, however, only fair to say that in the end these
tales produce a kind of unity of impression by accumu-
lated effect; and the conclusion, which relates the well-
known story of Ossian, Finn's son, left alone of all the

Fenians, an old man in the house of St. Patrick, lamenting the decay of the bright pagan world and the gloom of the new monkish faith, has a touch of genuine sublimity. When the saint bids him cry to God for mercy, the stalwart heathen can only speak of his dear regretted joys: "My story is sorrowful. The sound of your voice is not pleasant to me. I will cry my fill, but not for God, but because Finn and the Fianna are not living." And again, quaintly: "Without the cry of the hounds or the horns, without guarding coasts, without courting generous women; for all that I have suffered by the want of food, I forgive the King of Heaven in my will."

TWO POETS OF THE IRISH MOVEMENT

IF one were to ask Mr. W. B. Yeats what he considered the chief characteristic of the movement he so ably represents, no doubt the last word to come to him would be *defeat*, and yet, if properly considered, this so-called Gaelic Revival, this endeavour to resuscitate a bygone past and to temper the needs of the present to outworn emotions, is, when all is said, just that and nothing more—a movement of defeat. I say this with some confidence, because the visit of Mr. Yeats among us, to lecture as a guest of the Irish Literary Society, has led me to look through his successive volumes systematically, and I have been more than ever impressed by the gradual development in them of a sense of failure and decay rather than of mastery and growth. And the impression has saddened me a little; for I confess to have become somewhat wearied by the imperialistic arrogance of Kipling the great and the lesser Kiplings, and to have been ready to welcome the gentler Muse of the Irish poets who are so often contrasted with him. I had expected, indeed, " to hear a voice of lamentation out of the Golden Age," but what really came to my ears was more like an imitation of the bewildered wailings of decadence which ruled lately in France and which has swept with it not a few Englishmen such as Mr. Arthur Symons. Nothing can be further from the virile passion and pathos, the action and interknitting of strong characters in the ancient Irish literature, than this modern " Celtic phantasmagoria," to use Mr. Yeats's own words, " whose meaning no man has discovered, nor any angel revealed." I read the tremendous story of Deirdre in Lady Gregory's version of the Irish saga of Cuchulain, and I am filled with the sorrow of her lamentation as with one of the unforgettable sorrows of the world:

"I am Deirdre without gladness, and I at the end of my life; since it is grief to be without them, I myself will not be long after them."

After that complaint Deirdre loosed her hair, and threw herself on the body of Naoise before it was put in the grave and gave three kisses to him, and when her mouth touched his blood, the colour of burning sods came into her cheeks, and she rose up like one that had lost her wits, and she went through the night till she came to where the waves were breaking on the strand. And a fisherman was there and his wife, and they brought her into their cabin and sheltered her, and she neither smiled nor laughed, nor took food, drink, or sleep, nor raised her head from her knees, but crying always after the sons of Usnach.

I read this noble adaptation of old Irish passion, and then turn to Mr. Yeats, who attempts to express " the stir and tumult of defeated dreams " through the mouths of these same heroes of ancient song, and this, for an example, is what I find:

> Were you but lying cold and dead,
> And lights were paling out of the West,
> You would come hither, and bend your head,
> And I would lay my head on your breast;
> And you would murmur tender words,
> Forgiving me because you were dead;
> Nor would you rise and hasten away,
> Though you have the will of the wild birds,
> But know your hair was bound and wound
> About the stars and moon and sun.

Mr. Yeats has somewhere defined certain poems as an endeavour "to capture some high, impalpable mood in a net of obscure images," and no little part of his own verse might fall under the same definition. Too often he appears to strive after an exalted mysticism by giving the reins to loose revery, seeming, indeed, not to recognise any distinction between these two states of mind. The long tradition of defeat that overshadows his country has turned him, together with most of the other singers of a New Ireland, away from the cruel realities of their world and from the simple passions that control the impulsive energies of men into this Celtic twilight of defeated dreams. In the silence of this retreat from the world, in the hush that falls after the thunder and tumult of the passing war gods, one might look to hear the still small voice of that genuine mysticism which, alone of all poetic moods, has scarcely come to utterance in English poetry. This would seem to be the true field for these poets who are so open to impressions of patriotism and whose native land, dear in innumerable ways, has suffered so many a sad eclipse. Something of this higher mysticism was, perhaps, heard in Mr. Yeats's earlier poems, but no one can read his more recent productions without observing what may be called a defalcation of the mind. Instead of the true voice of the spirit, we hear the chattering of old women whose memory is troubled by vague and foolish superstitions; we perceive a poet of undoubted powers lending himself to the mystery mongering of a circle of morbid clerks; we listen to the revelations of wandering beggars and workhouse paupers as if they were apocalyptic in origin; we find a man gone out among the hills to track "every old dream that has been strong enough to fling the weight of the world from its shoulders," and we get from him idle ghost stories and babbling repetitions of old wives' tales. To me, at least, it is all rather sad, for I should be so willing to accept this vaunted symbolism as a true message from one who has beheld the vision. Is it too much to say that this is the poetry of defeat? The "fret," to use an expressive Irish word, is over him, and too long brooding on the sorrow of the land has brought him to a state perilously like an absconding of the intellect.

Were it not that Mr. Yeats stands as the leader of a group of young poets who show undoubted talent and who have just cause for attempting to form a school of poetry somewhat apart from the main current of English literature, there would be no reason for taking his delinquencies seriously. As it is, one resents this flaccid note in what might otherwise be a concord of subtle and exquisite music. As I have said, the real kinship of Mr. Yeats's present style is with that of Arthur Symons, himself a disciple of the French decadents; only one must add in justice that no taint of moral degeneration has appeared in the Irish writer—and that is much to concede to a decadent. It would be easy to set forth this kinship by parallel quotations; to show, for instance, how in both writers the looseness of ideas betrays itself unmistakably in a curious uncertainty of rhythm, wherein the accents hover weakly and dissolve into a fluttering movement utterly different from the marching order of the strong poets. There is one trick of both (though it is much more marked in Mr. Yeats) which may seem trivial, and yet does in some way connect itself with the total impression of their art. This is an insistence on the hair in describing women. Just why this habit should smack of decadence, is not quite clear to me, but the feeling it inspires is unmistakable. Out of curiosity I counted the number of allusions to hair in the few poems that make up Mr. Yeats's *Wind among the Reeds,*

and found they mounted up to twenty-three. It
is "the long dim hair of Bridget," or "the
shadowy blossom of my hair," or "passion-
dimmed eyes and long heavy hair," or "a
flutter of flower-like hair," or "dim heavy
hair," or the command to "close your eyelids,
loosen your hair." There is a fragile beauty
in these expressions, no doubt, but withal something troubling and unwholesome; one thinks
of the less chaste descriptions of Arthur Symons
or the morbid women of Aubrey Beardsley's
pencil rather than of the strong ruddy heroines
of old Irish story. The trait is significant of
much.

Yet I would not be held to deny the loveliness
of many of Mr. Yeats's poems; above all I have
respect for the pure patriotism that burns through
his language like a clear flame within a vase of
thinly chiselled alabaster, although I believe that
the specific aims of the Gaelic enthusiasts are
tragically misdirected. It may even be the half-
avowed consciousness of this fatal mistake that
has so emphasised the note of defeat in their verse.
At times this patriotic fervour enables Mr. Yeats
to catch the old haunting magic that Matthew
Arnold marked as the chief characteristic of Celtic
literature. So in one of his earlier poems he pictures the supernatural creatures that troubled the
men who were digging into the hill of the Sidhe
folk, and his words might stand with the best of
such passages in the *Cuchulain :*

> At middle night great cats with silver claws,
> Bodies of shadow, and blind eyes like pearls
> Came up out of the hole, and red-eared hounds
> With long white bodies came out of the air
> Suddenly, and ran at them and harried them.

One does not soon forget those "blind eyes like pearls." Elsewhere Mr. Yeats seems to be aware that the wanton revery of his muse may cut him off from the fellowship of the " great legion of Ireland's martyr roll ":

> Know that I would accounted be
> True brother of that Company,
> Who sang to sweeten Ireland's wrong,
> Ballad and story, rann and song.
>
> .   .   .   .
>
> Nor may I less be counted one
> With Davis, Mangan, Ferguson,
> Because to him who ponders well,
> My rhymes more than their rhyming tell
> Of the dim wisdoms old and deep,
> That God gives unto man in sleep.
> For the elemental beings go
> About my table to and fro.
> In flood and fire and clay and wind,
> They huddle from man's pondering mind;
> Yet he who treads in austere ways
> May surely meet their ancient gaze.

If this is the poetry of defeat, it still retains a vision of pure beauty that is not without a message for those whose ears ring with the din of loud materialistic songs. Nay, I am not prepared to say that the poet of failure has not his own

place in the chorus that cheers and soothes us
when, at rare intervals perhaps, we seek the consolation of verse.   How few of us there are who
do not feel at times the wan lethargy of defeat
steal upon us!   It is not easy amid the sordid business of life, even amid the strong calls of generous
action when these are heard, to pay heed to the
still small voice; and in our moods of dejection
there may perchance be some kinship to spiritual
things in this feeling of defeat, in this surrender
to the vague fleeting shadows that tremble on the
inner eye.   The sadness of these poems of Ireland
is justified to us then, and we recall the stanzas
of another poet, " in his misery dead," composed
on the theme of that strange phrase, " To weep
Irish ":

> The sadness of all beauty at the heart,
> The appealing of all souls unto the skies,
> The longing locked in each man's breast apart,
> Weep in the melody of thine old cries.
>
> Mother of tears! sweet Mother of sad sighs !
> All mourners of the world weep Irish, weep
> Ever with thee; while burdened time still runs,
> Sorrows reach God through thee, and ask for sleep.
>
> And though thine own unsleeping sorrow yet
> Live to the end of burdened time, in pain;
> Still sing the song of sorrow ! and forget
> The sorrow, in the solace, of the strain.

Lionel Johnson, too, wrote with the sorrow of
Ireland constantly in his heart, and he may be

called, in one sense, like most of the writers of this school, a poet of failure; but out of this defeat he won a firm station of the spirit, as may be seen in the verses just quoted, very different from the hazy dreamland of Mr. Yeats. His is the uplifted courage of Milton:

> What though the field be lost?
> All is not lost; the unconquerable will, . . .
> And what is else not to be overcome.

Mr. Johnson's death last year (1902), at the early age of thirty-five, was an irreparable loss to modern English literature, and took away from the little band of Gaelic enthusiasts the one writer who held his genius in perfect control. There is something pathetically aloof in the fragmentary story of his life as it reaches us through his friends. He was of Irish birth, but received his education at Winchester and Oxford, coming in his university years much under the influence of Pater. After his college days he resided chiefly in London, writing an occasional article of criticism and sending forth at intervals a poem of refined and scholarly taste. There was a notable delicacy, even sanctity, in his character, and " a seal upon him as of something priestly and monastic." Always, indeed, whether at his chambers in Clifford's Inn or elsewhere, he avoided the tumult of many people—though he loved London strangely —and lived the life almost of a recluse. Yet his warmth of affection for his friends never waned,

and they in return reverenced the zeal and purity
of his intellectual aims as if he were a man set
apart from the common familiarities of society.
He wrote nobly of friendship, linking it with his
most sacred aspirations:

> Each friend possesses, each betrays,
>   Some secret of the eternal things;
> Each one has walked celestial ways,
>   And held celestial communings.

And another poem, composed in his newly won
religious fervour—for he became in early manhood
a devout convert to the Roman Church—sanctifies
friendship almost as if it were a sacrament of the
faith:

A FRIEND

> His are the whitenesses of soul,
>   That Virgil had; he walks the earth
> A classic saint, in self-control,
>   And comeliness, and quiet mirth.
>
> His presence wins me to repose;
>   When he is with me, I forget
> All heaviness; and when he goes,
>   The comfort of the sun is set.
>
> But in the lonely hours I learn,
>   How I can serve and thank him best;
> *God ! trouble him; that he may turn*
>   *Through sorrow to the only rest.*

He himself had something in him of the classic
saint.   His intellect was trained in the learning

of Greece and Rome, and possessed the firmness
and wholesome clearness that we associate with
the word classic. But his body is described as
being, " elfin small and light," like De Quincey's,
and again as " fragile and terribly nervous."
Those who care to read more of the short tragedy
of his life, with its pathetic secret, and of his
death, may find it told in *The Month*, by Miss
Guiney in her sympathetic manner. It is one of
the pitiably sad and still heroic chapters of our
literary annals. "With all his deference," writes
Miss Guiney, " his dominant compassion, his
grasp of the spiritual and the unseen, his feet
stood foursquare upon rock. He was a tower of
wholesomeness in the decadence which his short
life spanned. He was no pedant and no prig.
Hesitations are gracious when they are unaffected,
but thanks are due for the one among gentler
critics of our passing hour who cared little to
'publish his wistfulness abroad.' " There lies the
difference. From the wistfulness, I had almost
said the sickliness, of Mr. Yeats who seeks relief
in wasteful revery, we pass to the sternly idealised
sorrow of Lionel Johnson, well knit with intellectual fibre, and we understand that imperious
victory in defeat which Milton personified in his
Satan, thinking more of his own state, one feels,
than of the fallen angel; we are made aware for
the moment of that hidden spirit within us which
triumphs in failure—the unconquerable will, and
what is else not to be overcome. It is good to

read such poetry; there is a fountain in it of consolation—and which of us in our passage through
the world does not need consolation?—and we
drink from it the refreshment of a great courage.
If I were asked to name the ode written in recent
years which exhibits the whitest heat of poetical
emotion expressed in language of the most perfect
and classical restraint, which conforms most
nearly to the great models of old, I should without hesitation name Mr. Johnson's *Ireland*. Even
in detached stanzas the beauty of the poem cannot be entirely lost:

> Thy sorrow and the sorrow of the sea
> Are sisters; the sad winds are of thy race;
> The heart of melancholy beats in thee,
> And the lamenting spirit haunts thy face,
> Mournful and mighty Mother ! who art kin
>   To the ancient earth's first woe,
> When holy Angels wept, beholding sin.
> For not in penance do thy true tears flow,
> Not thine the long transgression; at thy name,
>   We sorrow not with shame,
> But proudly; for thy soul is white as snow.

> .   .   .   .

> Proud and sweet habitation of thy dead !
> Throne upon throne, its thrones of sorrow filled;
> Prince on prince coming with triumphant tread,
> All passion, save the love of Ireland, stilled.
> By the forgetful waters they forget
>   Not thee, O Inisfail !
> Upon thy fields their dreaming eyes are set,

They hear thy winds call ever through each vale.
Visions of victory exalt and thrill
           Their hearts' whole hunger still;
High beats their longing for the living Gael.

.   .   .   .

Sweet Mother! in what marvellous dear ways
Close to thine heart thou keepest all thine own!
Far off, they yet can consecrate their days
To thee, and on the swift winds westward blown
Send thee the homage of their hearts, their vow
           Of one most sacred care;
To thee devote all passionate power, since thou
Vouchsafest them, O land of love! to bear
Sorrow and joy with thee.   Each far son thrills
           Toward thy blue dreaming hills,
And longs to kiss thy feet upon them, Fair!

One needs no drop of Irish blood in his veins to
feel the exaltation and minstrelsy of the poet's
mood.   One feels, too, the strange mingling of
passion and aloofness, of melancholy and triumph,
that speaks in almost every poem of his two slender
volumes.   I have contrasted his art with that of
Mr. Yeats; there is a certain fitness in quoting the
living poet's appreciation of his fallen compeer.
Lionel Johnson, he writes, " has made a world full
of altar lights and golden vestures and murmured
Latin and incense clouds and autumn winds and
dead leaves, where one wanders, remembering
martyrdoms and courtesies that the world has
forgotten.   His ecstasy is the ecstasy of combat,
not of submission to the Divine will; and even
when he remembers that ' the old Saints prevail,'

he sees the ' one ancient Priest' who alone offers
the Sacrifice, and remembers the loneliness of
the Saints. Had he not this ecstasy of combat, he would be the poet of those peaceful
and unhappy souls, who, in the symbolism of
a living Irish visionary, are compelled to inhabit when they die a shadowy island Paradise in the West." It is this "ecstasy of
combat," this triumph of defeat I choose to call
it, that, in my judgment, marks Mr. Johnson as
the one great, shall I say, and genuinely significant poet of the present Gaelic movement. Yet
how apt Mr. Yeats's criticism is may be seen from
the poem *Sertorius*, in which the vague longing
of these Irish dreamers is told in a parable of the
Roman leader in Spain. All the world knows the
story of Sertorius, and of his white hind which
the soldiers worshipped as an oracle of Diana.
Like the wistful visionaries of Ireland, his
thoughts turned in the hour of defeat to the
fabled islands of the Hesperides, where peace and
eternal hopes dwell in the misty West. How he
went not on that journey but was slain traitor-
ously at a banquet is recorded in history.

SERTORIUS

Beyond the Straits of Hercules,
Behold ! the strange Hesperian seas,
A glittering waste at break of dawn;
High on the westward plunging prow,
What dreams are on thy spirit now,
Sertorius of the milk-white fawn ?

Not sorrow to have done with home!
The mourning destinies of Rome
Have exiled Rome's last hope with thee;
Nor dost thou think on thy lost Spain.
What stirs thee on the unknown main?
What wilt thou from the virgin sea?

Hailed by the faithless voice of Spain,
The lightning warrior come again,
Where wilt thou seek the flash of swords,
Voyaging toward the set of sun?
Though Rome the splendid East hath won,
Here thou wilt find no Roman lords.

No Tingis here lifts fortress walls;
And here no Lusitania calls;
What hath the barren sea to give?
Yet high designs enchaunt thee still;
The winds are loyal to thy will;
Not yet art thou too tired to live.

No trader thou, to northern isles,
Whom mischief-making gold beguiles
To sunless and unkindly coasts;
What spirit pilots thee thus far
From the tempestuous tides of war,
Beyond the surging of the hosts?

Nay! this thy secret will must be.
Over the visionary sea,
Thy sails are set for perfect rest;
Surely thy pure and holy fawn
Hath whispered of an ancient lawn,
Far hidden down the solemn West.

A gracious pleasaunce of calm things;
There rose-leaves fall by rippling springs;
And captains of the older time,
Touched with mild light, or gently sleep,
Or in the orchard shadows keep
Old friendships of the golden prime.

The far seas brighten with grey gleams;
O winds of morning! O fair dreams!
Will not that land rise up at noon?
There, casting Roman mail away,
Age long to watch the falling day,
And silvery sea, and silvern moon.

Dreams! for they slew thee; Dreams! they lured
Thee down to death and doom assured;
And we were proud to fall with thee.
Now, shadows of the men we were,
Westward indeed we voyage here,
Unto the end of all the sea.

Woe! for the fatal, festal board;
Woe! for the signal of the sword,
The wine-cup dashed upon the ground;
We are but sad, eternal ghosts,
Passing far off from human coasts,
To the wan land eternal bound.

TOLSTOY; OR, THE ANCIENT FEUD BETWEEN PHILOSOPHY AND ART

THIS has been a century of strange conversions, and not least strange among these is Count Leo Tolstoy's abdication of an art in which he had won world-wide reputation for the rôle of prophet and iconoclast. " What is Art?" he has asked himself, and his published answer,[1] the outcome of fifteen years of meditation, is a denial of all that has made art noble in the past, and a challenge to those who seek to continue that tradition in the present. Furthermore he has put his theory into practice in a long and powerful novel, *Resurrection*.[2] Naturally such a renunciation on the part of an undisputed master in the craft caused no small commotion among poets and critics. Many of these, chiefly of the French school, shrugged their shoulders and smiled at a theory that would reject the works of Sophocles and Dante and Shakespeare as " savage and meaningless," and find in *Uncle Tom's Cabin* the acme of art toward

[1] *What is Art?* By Leo F. Tolstoy. New York: T. Y. Crowell & Co.

[2] *Resurrection.* By Leo F. Tolstoy. New York: Dodd, Mead & Co.

which the ages have been tending. Others have taken the quasi prophet more seriously, and with much ingenuity have pointed out the seeming flaws in his argument. Must I for my part confess that I have been chiefly impressed by the terrible and relentless logic of the book? It is easy to smile; it is easy to denounce the work as "literary nihilism put into practice by a converted pessimist." Pessimist and fanatic and barbarian Tolstoy may be, and to judge from his portrait alone he is all these; yet I know not how we shall escape his ruthless conclusions unless we deny resolutely his premises, and these are in part what our age holds as its dearest heritage of truth. Furthermore, his theoretic book may claim to be only the latest blow struck in a quarrel as old as human consciousness itself. Long ago Plato, himself a renegade from among the worshippers of beauty, could speak of "the ancient feud between philosophy and art," and to-day one of the barbarians of the North has delivered a shrewd stroke in the same unending conflict.

Least of all should we have expected to find in Greece this lurking antipathy between art and philosophy, for there, if anywhere in the world, truth and beauty seem to us to have walked hand in hand. It is curious that the school of Socrates, which did so much to introduce a formal divorce between these ideas, should have been so fond of the one word that more than any other expresses the intimate union of beauty and goodness.

Kalokagathia, beauty-and-goodness, "that solemn word in which even the gods take delight," was ever on their lips. In the beginning, no doubt, this strangely compounded term conveyed the simple thought still dear to our own youth when a fair face seems naturally and inevitably the index of a noble soul. That indeed is the ideal which we believe the truest gentlemen of Athens actually attained; we think we see it portrayed in the statues bequeathed to us by the land; it is at least the goal toward which Greek art ever strove as the reintegration of life. But after all we must confess that this harmony of the inner and the outer vision was but an ideal in Greece, such as has now and again glanced before other eyes,— only appearing not quite so fitfully there and approaching at times nearer the reality. Had it been anything more than a desire of the imagination, the history of the world would have been something quite different from the vexed pages of growth and decay which we now read. Perhaps, too, Joubert was not entirely wrong when he said that " God, being unable to bestow truth upon the Greeks, gave them poesy." Achilles, fair without and noble within, was the glory of the race; but too often the reality was like Paris, divinely beautiful and beloved of the goddess, but hollow at heart. From an early date the wise men of the land foresaw the threatened danger. Pythagoras, who descried the poets tortured in hell, was not the only prophet to denounce their travesty of the gods; nor was Solon the only sage who looked askance on the stage.

But Socrates, the first man of the Western world to attain to full self-consciousness, was the first also to ask seriously, What are truth and goodness? and what is beauty? And though in general he would deprive beauty of its peril, by reducing it to a mere matter of utility, yet at times he seems as a philosopher to have recognised its doubtful allurements. Xenophon reports an amusing conversation with his master on the nature of kissing, wherein Socrates in his usual style of badinage hints at this hidden peril. " Know you not," says he, " that this monster, whom you call beauty and youth, is more terrible than venomous spiders? These can sting only by contact, but that other monster injects his poison from a distance if a man but rest his eyes upon him." In another book we read Socrates's misgivings in regard to the current meaning of the word *kalokagathia*. He with his contemporaries had supposed that a necessary harmony existed between virtue and a man's outer semblance, until experience brought its cruel awakening. Beauty, which as a Greek he could not omit from the composition of a full man, became thenceforth for him, as for the rest of the world, mere grace of inner character, scarcely distinguishable from goodness itself. This idea is naïvely developed in a conversation with the country gentleman of the *Œconomicus*, where Socrates asks his old friend how despite his homely exterior he has won the reputation of uniting perfect beauty and goodness.

If we are a little surprised to hear the contemporary of Phidias and Sophocles speak doubtfully of the office of beauty, what shall we think of his disciple Plato, who was himself in youth a poet, and who in manhood was master of all styles, and able to drape in the robes of fancy the barest skeleton of logic? He, if any one, has given us " the sweet foode of sweetly uttered knowledge," and we further may say of him, with Sir Philip Sidney, " almost hee sheweth himselfe a passionate lover, of that unspeakable and everlasting beautie to be seene by the eyes of the minde, onely cleered by fayth"; and yet Plato knew and could avow that "to prefer beauty to virtue was the real and utter dishonour of the soul." I can imagine that to one bred on the visions of poetry and by birth a worshipper of all the fair manifestations of Nature, nothing could be more disconcerting than to follow the changes of Plato's doctrine in this regard. In the earlier dialogues physical comeliness is but a symbol of inner grace, a guide to lead us in the arduous and perilous ascent of the soul; and his theory of love was to become the teacher of idealism to a new world. In *The Republic* the cardinal virtues are blent into one perfect harmony of character so alluring as to seem the reflection in his mind of all the visual charm he had seen in Hellas. But even here his change

of attitude is apparent; this same dialogue contains that bitter diatribe against poetry and music
which would banish inexorably all the magicians
of art from his ideal state, because they draw the
mind from the contemplation of abstract truth to
dwell upon her deceptive imitations.   The world
has not forgotten and will never forget how these
greatest Athenians turned away their eyes from
what had given their land its splendid predomi-
nance.   Socrates's question, What is beauty? was
the "little rift within the lute," that was to widen
until the music of Greece became hushed for ever.

We may liken the texture of art to that floating
garment of gauze, inwoven with a myriad forms
and symbols, in which the goddess Natura was
wont to appear to the visionary eyes of the schoolmen: we may liken it to the clouds that drift
across the sky, veiling the effulgence of the sun
and spreading an ever variable canopy of splendour
between us and the unfathomed abyss: we may
better liken it to the curtain that hung in the
temple before the holy of holies; and the rending
of the curtain from top to bottom may signify a
changed aspect in the warfare of our dual nature.
A new meaning and acrimony enter into the conflict henceforth.   Christianity introduced, or at
least strongly emphasised, those principles that
were in the end to make possible such an utter revolt as Tolstoy's.   With the progress of the new
era, the feud between philosophy and art will take
on a thousand different disguises, appearing now

as a contest between religion and the senses, and again as a schism within the bosom of the Church itself. To the followers of Christ, the indwelling of divinity is no longer made evident by beauty of external form, for their incarnate deity came to them as one in whom there was "no form nor comeliness" nor any "beauty that we should desire him." Instead of magnanimity and magnificence the world shall learn to honour humility; a different sense shall be given to the word equality, and the individual soul will assume importance from its heavenly destiny, and not from its earthly force or impotence; the ambition to make life splendid shall be sunk in humanitarian surrender to the weak; the genial command of the poet, "Doing righteousness make glad your heart," shall be changed to the shrill cry of the monk, "But woe unto those that know not their own misery; and woe yet greater unto those that love this miserable and corrupted life!" Not that the old desire of loveliness shall be utterly routed from the world; but more and more it will be severed from the life of the spirit, and appear more and more as the seducer, and not the spouse, of the soul.

As in so many other things St. Augustine voices in this matter also the sentiment of the Christian world. He who in youth had written a treatise *On the Fit and the Beautiful*, turned after his conversion to bewail his unregenerate infatuation over the charms of Virgil. The grace of the

natural world became for him only a "snare of
the eyes"; and so fearful is he of the "delight of
the ears" that he hesitates to accept even the
singing in the church.

To the same horror of the lust of the eye and
the pride of life may be traced in part the anoma-
lous attitude of the Fathers and later churchmen
toward women. It was the mission of the new
faith to promulgate the distinctly feminine virtues
in place of the sterner ideals of antiquity,—love in
place of understanding, sympathy for justice, self-
surrender for magnanimity,—and as a consequence
the eternal feminine was strangely idealised, giving
us in religion the worship of the Virgin Mary,
and in art the raptures of chivalry culminating in
Dante's adoration of Beatrice. But there is a
darker side to the picture. Because the men of
the new faith could not acquiesce in any simple
life of the senses, woman must be either ethereal-
ised into an abstraction of religious virtues, or, if
taken humanly, must be debased as the bearer of
all the temptations of the flesh. She is the earthly
vision of heaven or hell,—unless to some more
human satirist she appears simply as purgatory.
It is painful to read the continuous libel of the
mediæval schoolmen upon woman; from St. Anthony down she is the real devil dreaded by the
pious, a personification of the *libido sentiendi*.

This same revolt from the senses reaches a dramatic crisis in the eighth century under Leo the
iconoclastic Emperor; and iconoclasm, though

largely the work of a single man, produced far-
reaching results in history, hastening the final
disruption of the East and the West, and estab-
lishing the Pope more firmly on his seat. It may
seem that Plato's philosophic feud with art has
assumed a grotesque disguise when championed
by rude fanatic mobs wreaking their vengeance
on altars and images; yet it is but the same
quarrel in a new and more virulent form. It is
significant, too, of an antagonism within the
Christian fold itself which even to this day has
not been fully allayed. The old dispensation had
forbidden the making of graven images; Christ
had declared that God should be worshipped
neither in Jerusalem nor in Samaria; his worship
was to be of the spirit alone. And it was to satisfy this negative suprasensuous side of religion
that the Byzantine Emperor instituted his reform.
He failed, but was at least a forerunner of the
Reformation which was largely a revolt of the
Northern races against the instinct of the South
to clothe abstract ideas in form and colour. Luther
was the great and successful iconoclast.

But no religious aspiration could entirely deaden
the appeal of the senses. During the heat of the
iconoclastic debate, John of Damascus had given
fervent expression to the soul's need of visible
symbols. " Thou perchance," he writes, " art
lifted up and set further apart from this material
world; thou walkest above this body as if borne
down by no weight of the flesh, and mayst despise

whatever thine eyes behold. But I, who am a
man and clothed in the body, desire to converse
with holy things in the body and to see them with
mine eyes.'' And again he asseverates that those
who wish to be united to God in the mind alone
should go further and take from the Church her
lamps, her sweet-smelling incense, her chanted
prayers, and the very sacraments which are of
material nature,—and all these things were indeed
to be swept away in good time. But in the meanwhile Christianity had produced its own legitimate form of art, different utterly from the brave
parade of paganism, yet not without its justifica-
tion. The artist did not seek for pure beauty, for
that intimate harmony of sense and spirit which
had been the ideal of Greece; matter is now constrained to express the humility, the ascetic dis-
dain, the spiritual aspiration and loneliness of the
soul. Yet one other, and perhaps the most essential, aspect of the faith, the humanitarian
sense of brotherhood and equality, must wait for
the nineteenth century for its complete utterance.

If the Reformation was but a prolongation of
the iconoclastic sentiment with certain new elements of moral and political antipathy added, the
Renaissance in the South was a deliberate attempt
to re-establish the old pagan harmony. But
something artificial and hollow soon showed itself
in the movement. The true balance was never
attained, or if attained was held but for a moment;
and the sensuous love of beauty, severed from the

deeper moral instincts of humanity, dragged out a spurious existence, until now it is seen in the most degraded forms of modern French art.

This is not the place to follow the conflict of our dual nature through all the ramifications of history. Those who wish to study it in its most dramatic moment may turn to the story of England in the seventeenth century, or read *John Inglesant*, where it developed into a romance of curious fascination. And to us of America at least the struggle of that period must always possess singular interest; for out of it grew the intellectual life of our nation, and even to-day the poverty of our art and literature is partly due to the fact that our strongest colonists brought with them only one faction of the endless feud.

For the feud is not settled and can never be settled while human nature remains what it is. To-day the man who approaches the higher intellectual life is confronted by the same question that troubled Plato. He who can choose without hesitation between art and religion, or between the new antinomy of literature and science, has climbed but a little way on the ladder of experience. There was a parable current among the Greeks, and still to be found in our modern school readers, which tells how the youthful Hercules in the pathway of life was met by two women who represented virtue and pleasure, and who bade him choose between the careers they offered. And it has often seemed to me that the fable

might be applied without much distortion to
many an ardent man who in his youth goes out
into the solitudes to meditate on the paths of ambition,—his choice lying not between virtue and
pleasure, but between the philosophic and the
imaginative life.   As he sits musing in some such
solitude of the spirit, we can discern two feminine
forms approach him, very tall and stately,— one
of them good to look upon and noble in stature,
clad in modest raiment, and with a brooding gaze
of austerity in her eyes as if troubled by no vision
of turbid existence; the other more radiant in face,
and richer and more alluring in form, with wide
open eyes that might be mirrors for all the de-
lightful things of nature, and dressed in a floating
transparent robe wherein are woven figures of
many strange flowers and birds.   She of the fluttering garment comes forward before the other,
and greets the youth effusively, and bids him follow her, for she will lead him by a pleasant path
where he shall suffer no diminution of the desires
of his heart, neither be withheld from the fulness
of earthly experience, but always he shall behold
a changing vision of wonder and beauty, and in
the end be received into the palace of Fame.
Here the youth asks by what name she is known,
and she replies: " My friends call me Fancy, and
I dwell in the meadows of Art, but my enemies
call me Illusion."   In the meanwhile the other
woman has drawn near, and now she says to the
young man: " Nay, follow me rather, and I will

show you the true value of life. I will not deceive you with cunning seductions of the eye and ear that lead only to distraction in the end. The road in which I shall guide you lies apart from the vanities and triumphs of earthly hopes; the way of renunciation will seem hard to tread at first, but slowly a new joy of the understanding will be awakened in you, born of a contempt for the fleeting illusions of this world, and in the end you shall attain to another and higher peace that passeth understanding. I am named Insight, and by some my home is called Philosophy and by others Religion." I can fancy that some such parting of the ways has come to many of those who by choosing resolutely have won renown as artists or seers. I can believe that some who have elected the smoother path have even in the full triumph of success felt moments of regret for the other life of ascetic contemplation.

More than one great artist, to be sure, has vaunted the perfect efficacy of his craft to satisfy the human soul; more than one poet has published his Defence of Poetry, and declared with Shelley that "the great instrument of moral good is the imagination, and poetry administers to the effect by acting upon the cause." Even Horace has written his " melius Chrysippo et Crantore "; and no doubt in the last analysis the poets are right. Yet still the haunting dread will thrust itself on the mind, that in accepting, though it be but as a symbol, the beauty of the world, we

remain the dupes of a smiling illusion. And
something of this dread seems to rise to the surface now and again in the works of those who
have penetrated most deeply into art and life. So
the pathos of Shakespeare's sonnets may be chiefly
due to the effect upon us of seeing a great and
proud genius humiliated before a creature of the
court. Not all his supremacy of art could quite
recompense the poet for his uneasiness before the
fine assurance of noble birth, or cover completely
the "public means which public manners breeds";
but gathering the hints here and there in the sonnets and comparing them with the scattered passages of disillusionment in the plays, I seem to
read a deeper discontent with the artistic life, a
feeling that he had not been faithful to his own
truer self.

> Alas, 't is true I have gone here and there
>   And made myself a motley to the view,
> Gor'd mine own thoughts, sold cheap what is
>   most dear,
>   Made old offences of affections new;
> Most true it is that I have look'd on truth
>   Askance and strangely,—

he writes in one of the sonnets; and may it not
be that this petulant discontent is partly responsible for his failure to care for the preservation of
his works?

Still more striking is the attitude of Michael
Angelo in old age toward the occupation of his

life. I trust I may be pardoned for giving at length a translation of the well-known sonnet in which the supreme artist turns at last for consolation to a Love above his earthly love:

After the seas tempestuous, lo, I steer
  My fragile bark with all my hopes aboard
  Unto that common haven where the award
Of each man's good and evil must appear.
Wherefore the phantasie I held so dear,—
  That made of art my idol and my lord,—
  Too well I know is all with errors stored,
And man's desires that bind him helpless here.
Those amorous thoughts that lightly moved my
        breast,
  What do they now when near two deaths I toss,
    One certain here, one threatening yet above?
Not painting now nor sculpture lulls to rest;
  The soul hath turned to that diviner Love
Whose arms to clasp us opened on the cross.

It would be absurd to compare the words and actions of Tolstoy with the great names already cited, were it not that the Russian novelist is a true spokesman of certain tendencies of the age. To be sure, the religious aspect of the ancient feud has for the present been much obscured, and the most notable conflict to-day is undoubtedly between the imagination and the analytical spirit of science. But within the realm of art itself a curious division has appeared which is still intimately connected with the religious instinct though in a new form; and on this present aspect of the

question the career of Tolstoy will be seen to throw
an instructive light.

The humanitarian side of Christianity had been
more or less concealed throughout the Middle
Ages by the anxiety for personal salvation. In
such a work as the *Imitation* the brotherhood of
mankind taught by the Apostles was quite smothered by a refined and spiritual form of egotism;
nor can we imagine a St. John declaring, "As
often as I have gone forth among men, I have returned home less a man." Both the isolation
peculiar to such an ideal and the spirituality
which it had in common with earlier Christianity
were impossible after the humanism of the Renaissance and the scepticism of the eighteenth century.
Instead of these many things conspired together
at the opening of the nineteenth century to emphasise that other phase of Christianity, the belief in the divine right of the individual and
the brotherhood of man. Deprive this belief
of spirituality, and add to it a sort of moral impressionism which abjures the judgment and
appeals only to the emotions, and you have the
humanitarian religion of the age. And naturally
the most serious art of the times has reflected this
movement.

So, for example, Wordsworth has been much
lauded as the high priest of Nature, whereas in reality the important innovation introduced by him
into English poetry is not his appreciation of Nature but his humanitarianism, his peculiarly senti-

mental attitude toward humble life. This, and not any feeling of the exigencies of art,—for his later work shows that he had no such artistic sensitiveness,—is the true source of his determination to employ "the language of conversation in the middle and lower classes of society." Art is no longer the desire of select spirits to ennoble and make beautiful their lives, but an effort to touch and elevate the common man and to bring the proud into sympathy with the vulgar. And this, too, explains Wordsworth's choice of such humble themes as *Michael*, and *The Idiot Boy*, and a host of the same sort. The genius of Wordsworth was in this prophetic of what was to be the deepest religious instinct of the age; and if this instinct has as yet produced few great poetic names besides that of Wordsworth himself and Shelley, yet the strength of such a novel as Miss Wilkins's *Jerome* and the public reception of such a poem as *The Man with the Hoe* (*horresco referens*) show perhaps how deep a hold the feeling is to have on the literature of the immediate future.

As a revolt against this ideal and a feeble prolongation of the aims of the Renaissance, the contrary school of Art for Art's sake has arisen, in which beauty, like a bodiless phantom of desire, lures the seeker ever further and further from real life, weaning him from the healthier aspiration of his time, and only too often plunging him into the mire of acrid sensuality. The Goncourts in their Journal have admirably expressed the wasteful

14

illusion of this search: "Le tourment de l'homme
de pensée est d'aspirer au Beau, sans avoir jamais
une conscience fixe et certaine du Beau." We
wonder to what hidden recess of the world the old
Greek vision of the union of beauty and virtue has
flown, and if that too is only an empty phantom
of the mind.

Such, it seems to me, is the present form of the
ancient feud between philosophy and art, now
waged within the field of art itself—if this am-
biguous use of the word may be pardoned. The
complexity of life of course does much to obscure
the contrast of these two tendencies, but it is natural that a man of Tolstoy's race, with his bar-
baric use of logic and his intemperate scorn of the
golden mean, should see the contrast in its naked-
ness and fling himself into the battle with fanatic
ardour. But perhaps he himself does not understand, and others may not at first perceive, how
much he has in common with the decadent artists
whom he attacks, and how the true opponent of
that tendency would be the man of sufficient insight to present to the world a new and adequate
ideal of the beautiful.

Tolstoy's definition of art is very clear and consistent:

Art [he maintains] is not, as the metaphysicians say,
the manifestation of some mysterious Idea of beauty, or
God; it is not . . . a game in which man lets off
his excess of stored-up energy; it is not the expression of
man's emotion by external signs; it is not the production

of pleasing objects; and, above all, it is not pleasure; but it is a means of union among men, joining them together in the same feelings, and indispensable for the life and progress toward well-being of individuals and of humanity. . . . To evoke in one's self a feeling one has experienced, and . . . so to transmit that feeling that others may experience the same feeling—this is the activity of art.

Tolstoy's position is precise, but in the end does he offer any ideal more than the decadent who seeks beauty as a refined, or even gross, means of pleasure, or than the pure humanitarian who sympathises with mankind without any ulterior spiritual insight? I cannot see how the reformer has passed beyond mere impressionism, and impressionism is one of his most hated foes. The end of art for him is simply to transmit feeling from man to man. He distinctly denies the office of the intellect in art, ascribing this to science, and he has left no room for the higher appeal to the will. The strength of the impression conveyed is the final criterion of excellence. The artist is amenable to no laws, and his work is not subject to interpretation or to criticism. " One of the chief conditions of artistic creation," he says, "is the complete freedom of the artist from every kind of preconceived demand." The whim of the individual is the supreme arbiter of taste. Sympathy, and not judgment, is the goal of culture. Nor does the old notion of beauty suffer less at his hands. To him the Greeks were but savages (it is a Russian who speaks), and their conception of the *kalokagathia* the result of sheer ignorance. There is no ideal which beauty serves, and its application to character is a mere abuse of words. To him, as to the decadents and the humanitarians, beauty is no more than a name for pleasure, and no explanation can be given why any object should please one man and displease another. So far we are on ground common to both humanitarianism and decadent art; but at this point occurs the division, and Tolstoy as a true schismatic throws himself on one side with the whole vehemence of his nature.

Seeing that the pursuit of beauty as something unconnected with character is a most insidious danger, and that art which possesses such an aim must inevitably become corrupt, he cuts the Gordian knot by discarding beauty altogether as one cf the elements of art. In place of it he would complete his theory of impressionism and the divine right of the individual by adding the moral intention which makes of these a religion. The old ideal of art had been sought in the union of the higher intellect and the aspirations of the will touched with emotion; and the final court of appeal was the taste of the man who had attained to the most perfect harmony of culture and to the fullest development of character. Tolstoy, on the contrary, carries his doctrine of individualism to the extreme. If the light treatment of so grave a subject may be pardoned,

He is the same as the Chartist who spoke at a meeting in
    Ireland,
" *What, and is not one man, fellow men, as good as
    another?* "
" *Faith,*" replied Pat " *and a deal better too!* "

Some criterion·of value he must have, and to find
this he turns to the judgment of the common
Russian peasant.   Nothing gives a better idea of
the change of civilisation than to compare Tolstoy's constant reference of art to the simple un-
tutored countryman, with the attitude of a man
like Pindar in the old Greek days, or with the
contempt of our Elizabethans for "the breath that
comes from the uncapable multitude;" for it must
be remembered that, after all, the Russian fanatic
is a man of the age, and that hidden in the heart
of each of us lies this same curious deference to
the untrained individual.   And in spite of this individualism,—or should we say in consequence of
it?—Tolstoy has attained his own conception of
universality as a basis for art.   It was formerly
the belief of the sages that by ascending the ladder
of intellectual experience a man might leave behind the desires and emotions in which his
personal life was bound up, and reach a purer atmosphere where only his truer universal self could
breathe.   And this obscurely and dimly was the
belief of the poet.   But Tolstoy would find the
universal by descending.   Art has nothing to do
with the intellect or with the will, or yet with
the exclusive emotions of a falsely isolated and

corrupted aristocracy, but appeals to the heart of
the humblest man, in whom the universal feelings
of humanity have not been covered over by culture
or luxury.   At least, as a revolt against the ex-
clusiveness of art for art's sake, this acceptance
of humanitarianism in its crudest form is a real
advance.   "The feeling of pride, the feeling of
sexual desire, and the feeling of weariness of life,"
are indeed not the true themes of art, and better
than these are "humility, purity, compassion,
love."   "Art," he says, "is not a pleasure, a
solace, or an amusement; art is a great matter;"
and we may forgive him much for that trumpet
call.   Art is indeed to him the handmaid of religion.   Of the spiritual quest of the individual
soul to sever himself from the world and to lose
himself in communion with God, little or nothing
remains: the very words sound meaningless in our
ears.   Let us not deceive ourselves: our religion
is, as Tolstoy states, "the new relation of man to
the world around him;" and in the effort to escape
by means of humility and universal sympathy
from the anarchy and selfishness of individualism,
art, regarded as the transmission of feeling from
man to man, may be a great force.   It thus becomes with science one of the two organs of human progress, science pertaining to the intellect
and art dealing with the interchange of emotions.
Progress to Tolstoy, as to the rest of his generation, is the battle-cry of the new faith, for "religious perception is nothing else than the first

indication of that which is coming into existence."
If you ask him toward what far-off divine event
this progress tends, he will answer with the closing words of his book, the "brotherly union
among men." Nor, until some ulterior goal is
proclaimed, can I see that the humanitarianism of
Tolstoy or of any other doctrinaire saves us from
this vicious circle of attempting to unite men for
the mere sake of union.

And in the case of Tolstoy this humanitarian
religion is marred by a stain that marks it peculiarly as a falling away from the real doctrine
of Christ on which he builds as on a foundation.
He claims to announce to a forgetful age the true
Gospel of Jesus, and the solemnity and undoubted
sincerity of his appeal have startled many hearers
from their apathy. They hear the very speech
of Christ on his lips and wonder whether after all
this humanitarianism of the day is the perfect and
purified revival of the mission preached by the
Messiah to the Old World which could not understand him. They hear the very speech of Christ,
yet their hearts are only troubled by what they
hear and no peace of conviction follows. They
are torn by the diversity of their feelings, and,
finding no flaw in the pitiless logic of the prophet,
are ready often to deny the authority of the Master
whose words he repeats.

Count Tolstoy accepts without reservation the
plain precepts of the Gospel, and demands our
adherence to the strict letter of the law. This

may be well, although possibly it denotes something of the false logic of fanaticism to dwell so persistently on the one command, " Resist not evil." But deeper than the commands lies the spirit of Christ; and he who follows the law of the Gospel without heeding the spirit, wherein does he differ from the Pharisees of the old dispensation whom Christ so vehemently denounced?

If you ask in what respect Tolstoy misses the heart of true religion and of Christ, I would reply in the words of a famous Frenchwoman, " *La joie de l'esprit en marque la force* "—the joy of the spirit is the measure of its force. It may seem trifling to confront the solemn exhortation of a prophet with the words of Ninon de l'Enclos, whose chief claim on our memory is the scandalous story of her grandson, who killed himself on discovering that he had fallen in love unwittingly with his own grandmother; and yet I know not where a saner criticism could be found of the arrogant dogmatism of this Russian bigot. There is no joy in Tolstoy, and lacking joy he lacks the deepest instinct of religion. I know that here and there a sentence, or even a page, may be quoted from Tolstoy that sounds as if he had discovered joy in his new faith, and I know that he repeats volubly the glad tidings that are said to have made the angels sing as they never sang before; but it needs no more than a glance at the rigid, glaring eyes of the old man to feel that the soul within him feeds on bitter and uncharitable thoughts, and it needs but a little familiarity with his later work in fiction to learn that the ground of his spirit is bitterness and denunciation and despair.

It is natural that a writer of Tolstoy's gloomy convictions should deny the validity of beauty and should call the Greeks ignorant savages because they believed in beauty. His own later work shows an utter absence of the sense of beauty and joy. The drama called *La Puissance des Ténèbres*—I do not know that it has ever been translated into English—is one of the most revolting and heart-sickening productions of the past century. The imagination of the author has apparently dwelt on unclean objects until it has become crazed with a mingled feeling toward them of attraction and repulsion.

Count Tolstoy takes his law of righteousness from the Sermon on the Mount, and that is well; but he has forgotten the song of joy that runs like a golden thread through that discourse—" Blessed are they that mourn; for they shall be comforted. . . . Rejoice, and be exceeding glad." Out of the preaching of Christ proceeds the wonderful and beautiful lesson of the fowls of the air and of the lilies of the field; out of the preaching of Tolstoy comes the loathsome *Powers of Darkness*. Or, if we look for a more modern instance, we may read the *Fioretti* of St. Francis of Assisi, than whom no one has trod nearer to the footsteps of Christ. The parables and poems of St. Francis

are all aglow with passionate joy and tenderness
and beauty.

I do not mean that sorrow and denunciation are
banished from the teaching of Christ. But the
sorrow of Christ is not the uncharitable cry alone
of one whose spirit has been wounded by seeing
wrong and injustice in the world. Does it need a
prophet to tell us the times are out of joint? Nor
is it the anguish of a spirit that has retreated bitterly upon itself because the world does not re-
spond to his own personal demands. It is rather
the brooding pity of one who sees that the fashion
of this world passeth away, and that rich and poor
alike are in the bondage of sin. There is in him
neither the rancor of class hatred nor the wail of
personal disillusion. The world is dark to him
because it lies outside the great and wonderful
radiance of the kingdom of heaven. If I read
aright the fragmentary record of Christ's life it
was more filled with the joy of spiritual insight
than with the bitterness of earthly despair.

And this is not the nature of Christianity alone,
but of true faith wherever found. We hear much
of the pessimism of Buddha, and Schopenhauer is
supposed to have sucked thence the poison of his
philosophy; but in reality the doctrine of Buddha
in its pure form is one of unspeakable gladness.
He dwelt much on the transitory nature of this
world and on the misery of human life, but he
dwelt far more on the ineffable peace and joy of
deliverance. There is the pessimism of one whose

vision is wholly downward, and who sees only
the bleakness of earthly life; there is another so-
called pessimism of one whose vision is ever upward, and to whom, therefore, the world seems a
clog on his progress toward perfect happiness, and
such, if it be pessimism at all, is the pessimism of
Buddha.   Only a reader familiar with the Buddhist books can have any notion of the overwhelming spirit of gladness and simple charity that
pervades them.   There is in one of them the story
of a prince who is converted and leaves the luxury
of a palace to join the brotherhood; and we are
told that in the night-time the brothers heard him
walking outside in the grove and crying to himself, *Aho ! Aho !* for his joy was so great that he
could not sleep.

In a word, the sadness of true religion is negative, the joy positive. Faith is the deliberate
turning of the eye from darkness to light.   If the
words of the preacher close the doors in our breasts
and bring to us a contracted feeling of depression,
we may know that his denunciation of the world
is because the world has turned to ashes in his
mouth and not because he has attained to any
true vision of the peace of the spirit.

It is because there is no note of spiritual joy in
Tolstoy when he speaks from his own heart and
lays aside the borrowed jargon of Christianity,
it is because there is in him only the bitterness
of a great and smitten soul, it is because there
is in him no charity or tenderness, but only the

bleakness of disillusion, that he must be counted
in the end an enemy to faith and not an upbuilder
of faith.

I have dwelt thus at length on Tolstoy's theory
of the new art and on his religion of humanitarianism from which this theory springs rather than
on his practice of art as shown in the novel *Resurrection*, because his theoretic writing seemed to me
more fruitful and suggestive, and because—let me
confess it—the novel has awakened in my mind a
repugnance strongly at variance with the eulo-
gistic reception it has gained at large. There is
undoubtedly superabundant force in the book;
there is the visual power, so common in Russian
novels, which compels the reader to see with his
own eyes what the author describes; there is
profound skill of characterisation, clothing the
persons of the story in flesh and blood; but with
all this, what have we in the end but " the ex-
pense of spirit in a waste of shame " ?

It would be an easy task to point out how perfectly the novel follows the author's theory, and
how completely it presents him as a decadent
with the humanitarian superimposed. There is
the same utter inability to perceive beauty as connected with a healthy ideal of character, and a
consequent repudiation of beauty altogether.
There is the same morbid brooding on sex which
lent so unsavoury a reputation to the *Kreutzer
Sonata*. It should seem that the author's mind
had dwelt so persistently and intensely on this

subject as to induce a sort of erotic mania taking
the form at once of a horrid attraction and repulsion. We are sickened in the same way with endless details of loathsome description that are made
only the more repellent by their vividness; nor
can I see how the fascination of such scenes as
the trial and the prison can be based on any
worthier motive than that which collects a crowd
about some hideous accident of the street. It is
not science, for it is touched with morbid emo-
tionalism. It is not true art, for it contains no
element of elevation. It is not right preaching,
for it degrades human nature without awakening
any compensating spiritual aspiration. It is,
when all has been said, the same spirit of unclean
decadence as that which led Baudelaire to write
his stanzas on *Une Charogne*, and it classes Tolstoy in many respects with that corrupt school
which he so heartily detested. The travesty of
life presented in the book may be explained—I do
not know—by the barbarous state of Russian
civilisation. The coarseness of details, however,
may well be charged to the individual mind of the
man who while describing in his memoirs the
burial of his own mother dilates on the odour of
the body. This is not a pleasant fact to mention,
but is in itself worth a volume of argument.
Christianity was thrust upon the Northern heathen at the point of sword and pike: it should seem
as if this propagator of humanitarianism was bent
on making converts by trampling under foot all

the finer feelings and fairer instincts, all the decorum and suavity, of human nature.

Such, at present is the most notable phase of the ancient feud, so far at least as it concerns literature; and from the horns of this dilemma—the mockery of art for art's sake on one side, and on the other the dubious and negative virtue of the humanitarians—I find no way of escape, unless the world discovers again some positive ideal which beauty can serve. And if you say that this conflict is only one phase of an ever changing and never solved antinomy of human nature, and that the conception of the good and beautiful was an empty word of the philosophers, certainly I shall not attempt to answer in terms of logic, for I myself have been too long haunted by a similar doubt. And yet I seem to see dimly and figuratively the shadow of a solution. Call it a dream if you will; but what else was the vision of Jacob when he lay asleep and beheld a ladder stretching from the earth to the sky? or the journey of Dante up the Mountain of Purgatory and from planet to planet? or Dionysius's doctrine of the hierarchy of angels and principalities and powers reaching in unbroken succession from man to the Supreme Being?

Somewhere in that same visionary land I beheld a great mountain, whose foot was in a valley of eternal shadows, and whose head was lost in the splendour of the pure empyrean. At first the eye was bewildered and could see only the strange contrast of the gloom below and the whiteness above; but as I looked longer, I discerned a path that stretched from one to the other up the whole length of the slope, uniting them by gradual changes of light and shade. On this pathway were countless human souls, some toiling upward, others lightly descending, but none pausing, for there seemed to be at work within them some principle of unrest which forever impelled them this way or that. And their journey was a strange and mystic pilgrimage, through ever varying scenes, between the deep abyss far below, where monstrous creatures like the first uncertain births of Chaos wallowed in the slime and darkness, and high above the regions made dim with excess of light, where in the full noonday figures of transcendent glory seemed to move. And I saw that of all the pilgrims a few lifted their eyes aloft to the great white light, and were so ravished by its radiance that the objects before their feet were as if they did not exist. And of these few one here and there pressed on valiantly and in time was himself rapt from view into the upper radiance; but the others were blinded by the light, and lost their foothold, and were hurled headlong into the loathsome valley. And I saw a few others whose eyes turned by some horrid fascination to the abyss itself, and thither they rushed madly, heedless of every allurement by the way. But by far the greater number kept their regard fixed modestly on the path just above or below, according as the spirit within led them to ascend or descend. And these seemed to walk ever in a kind of earthly paradise; for the light, streaming down from the empyrean and tempered to their vision by wont, fell upon the trees by the roadside and on the flowering shrubs innumerable and on the mountain brooks, and gilded all with wonderful and inexpressible beauty. And those that gazed above were filled with such joy at the fresh world before them that they climbed ever upward and never rested, for always some scene still fairer lured them on. And as they climbed, the light grew brighter and more clear, and the path more beautiful and easier to ascend, and so without seeming toil or peril they too passed from sight. But those others who cast their eyes on the pathway below were drawn in the same way by the beauty of the scene where the golden light glanced on the trees; and with much ease and satisfaction to themselves they paced down and still downward, following the shifting vision and dallying with pleasure on the way, and never observed how the light was growing dimmer and the road more precipitous, until losing balance they were thrown headlong into the noisome valley.

So the division and conflict of human nature appeared to me in a parable; but whether the vision had any meaning or was only an idle fancy, I do not know.

THE RELIGIOUS GROUND OF HUMANI-
TARIANISM

No writer of the present day has discussed the
intricate problem of social evolution more logically
than Mr. Mallock, and even his enemies will admit that his *Aristocracy and Evolution* presents a
strong plea in favour of the so-called " great-man
theory" against the claims of socialism and of
those theories generally that would sink the individual in the mass. Mr. Mallock's argument, reduced to the briefest terms, is simply this: Social
science attempts to answer two distinct sets of
questions; and one set—namely, the speculative
—it has answered with great success; it has failed
only in attempting to answer practical questions.

The phenomena with which it has dealt suc-
cessfully are phenomena of social aggregates considered as wholes; but the practical problems of
to-day, with which it has dealt unsuccessfully,
arise out of the conflict between different parts of
the same aggregate. Social science has failed as
a practical guide because it has not recognised
this distinction. The conflict between the parts
of an aggregate arises from inequalities of position. These social inequalities are partly due to

circumstances; but most people will admit that congenital inequalities in talent have much to do with these social inequalities. The condemnation of the great-man theory is a removal of all congenital inequalities from the field of study. It may be asked what place the great man has in an exclusively evolutionary theory of progress. The reply is that the fittest survivor is not the same as the great man. He plays a part in progress, but not the same part. The fittest men, by surviving, raise the general level of the race and promote progress in this way. The great man promotes progress by being superior to his cotemporaries. The movement of progress is double; one movement being very slow, the other rapid. The survival of the fittest causes the slow movement; the rapid movement is caused by the great man. Mr. Mallock's argument then proceeds to show how the great man—that is, the man of exceptional abilities in any one field, often a very narrow field—working through the law of competition renders the labour of the masses more efficient by his directive power, and thus increases the general well-being. And the only possible incentive to induce the great man to enter into this arena of material competition is the material rewards such as he now receives in the world.

It is of course a manifest injustice to condense the argument of a large volume, with all its wealth of illustration and rebuttal, to the limits of a paragraph; but such an act may be justified

in the present case because our purpose is to attempt neither the refutation nor the support of
socialism on economic grounds, but to examine
the question from quite a different point of view.
To our mind Mr. Mallock's theory is correct so
far as it goes, and we presume that most persons
of intelligence will admit the strength of his
reasoning if only economic grounds are considered
and, what is more important, if only the competi-
tive side of human nature is taken into account.
But just here we see the weak point of his argument. A person may well retort: Mr. Mallock's
theory, as you maintain, is true so far as it goes;
but it professedly touches only the worldly and
materialistic element of human nature. The law
of competition will necessarily produce such a
state of society as he describes; but the law of
competition, while perfectly valid in the lower
stages of civilisation, takes no account of what
may be called the religious or humanitarian instinct of man; and it is just this higher instinct
which introduces a new factor into human progress and makes possible the claims of socialism.
I say " religious or humanitarian instinct " pur-
posely, for it must be perfectly clear to any one
who looks abroad that religion to-day, so far as it
is a vital force, has very little to do with the salvation of individual souls and very much to do
with the regeneration of society as an organised
body. The brotherhood of man is the real religious dogma of the times. We wish to consider

briefly the force of this religious ground of socialism,—we should rather say humanitarianism, for
our concern is not with the specific political pro-
gramme of the socialists, properly so-called, but
with that ever-growing belief in the equality and
brotherhood of man which is equally responsible
for the nihilism of Tolstoy and the collectivism
of Karl Marx. If these claims are found to be
empty, it should seem that there remains for us
only to put away our dream of a regenerated society and of universal happiness, and to make the
best of the old order of things where justice seems
to our blinded vision to walk hand in hand with
the unequal fates.

And first of all it is necessary to examine more
carefully what is meant by the religious instinct
and to separate it from misleading overgrowths;
for evidently Christianity—to confine ourselves
for the moment to that form of belief—as taught
and practised to-day is a mingling of the religious
instinct with worldly policy. We mean nothing
invidious by worldly policy; but simply that the
religion of Christ, as it spread and became a
factor of civilisation, necessarily assumed a formal
policy and government—that it became a Church.
Neither in its Catholic nor in its Protestant form
has the Church lent itself to any promulgation or
protection of socialistic ideas of equality; and for
this reason the organised Church has been bitterly attacked by Socialists and social reformers
generally—most bitterly of all perhaps by Tolstoy,

who finds in it the ultimate cause of the wide-spread misery which the new acceptance of human brotherhood is to annul.   Indeed many Christians—and among them Tolstoy—assert that the organised Church stands in direct opposition to the plain teaching of Jesus, and that the chief need of the world to-day is to throw off these outer trappings of worldliness and to approach once more the original message of the Gospel. We are compelled, then, to disregard the policy of the Church, whether Catholic or Protestant, and to turn back to the pure voice of religion, which in the words of the great prophets appeals more or less authoritatively to the hearts of all men; for here, if anywhere, lies the only valid basis of that much-vaunted regenerating belief in the brotherhood and equality of men.   There can certainly be no surer and clearer way of discovering the oracles of this pure religion than by going to the words and example of Christ himself.   For the Christian this will be sufficient; for those of more questioning mind it may be proper to rein-force the teaching of Christ with the doctrine of Buddha.   He would be a rash man who should seek the mandates of religion outside of the realm in which these two greatest apostles of the West and of the East stand in concord.

At the outset of any attempt to discover the actual doctrine of Christ we are, however, met by a difficulty which must be frankly confessed and set down for whatever weight it may have.   Only

those who have gone to the Gospels without any
preconvictions of what they were to find know
how hard it is to discover the real position of
Christ. Single texts may be quoted, and indeed
have been quoted, to justify every variety of
creed; and I can see no way through the difficulties except to form an opinion from the general
consensus of Christ's acts and words.

It will help us if we discriminate among the
various elements of religion that enter into Christianity. Thus there is one phase of Christianity
which may be called the purely spiritual and
which it possesses with all higher cults. This
phase cannot better be expressed than in the
three words of St. Paul, *Faith*, *Hope*, and *Love*.
We are not here dealing with faith in a peculiar
dogma or person which may vary with varying
creeds, but with that faculty of the mind or soul
which turns instinctively to the things of the
spirit. And so in regard to hope, we mean simply
a state of joyous trust that somehow to the faithful all things in the end shall be good. And in
love we refer to no specific commands, but to that
sympathetic attitude of the observing soul which
is ready to accept and make a portion of its own
life the joys and sorrows of the world. It is at
bottom the desire of the soul to become one with
all it perceives akin to itself. These three form
the spiritual basis of all religion; and it is not
necessary to say how abundantly they are held
forth in the Gospels. But faith, hope, and love,

in this spiritual sense, have no direct bearing on the social question we are here considering. They are the fountainhead of Christianity, as of every religion, and flow down through all its manifestations; but they are of the spirit and not of this world. Even love, which at first might seem corroborative of humanitarian equality and is no doubt so interpreted, is in this spiritual sense a state of mind, not a rule of action. To do what is best for our neighbour, we must first be told what is best for him. And besides it applies as much to our feeling toward the dumb beasts as to our fellow-men.

And so at the other end of Christianity there lies a law which is common practically to humanity and which has no bearing on the question at issue. This is that universal code of prohibitive morality found in the Decalogue and in large part repeated and reinforced by Christ: Thou shalt not kill, Thou shalt not steal, etc.

But between these two extremes of spiritual outreaching and negative morality lies a common ground where the two orders meet together and produce a body of positive or spiritual morality which bears directly on constructive sociology. It is this ground that we are to investigate more narrowly in the doctrine of Christ.

If we turn to the Sermon on the Mount, which surely represents the teaching of Christ in its purest form, we are met in the beginning by the promulgation of a virtue distinctly medial in

character between the aspirations of the spirit and
the prohibitions of the flesh.   This is that virtue
of humility so often enounced by Christ and so
strikingly exhibited in his own life: Blessed are
the poor in spirit; Blessed are they that mourn;
Blessed are the meek!   It would be quite super-
fluous to dwell at length on this teaching of the
Son of Man, who came not to be ministered unto
but to minister, and who suffered voluntarily the
humiliation of the cross.   He never ceased to declare that he who would save his life should lose
it, and that he who would be first should be last.
Probably the one feature that most radically distinguishes Christianity from other religions is this
peculiar emphasis and reiteration of the lesson of
humility.   Something very much akin to it in its
results may be found elsewhere, notably in Buddhism as we shall see; but nowhere else has the
high formulative virtue just the same mark of
personal poignancy which is felt in Christian
humility.

Closely related to humility and following it as
an immediate corollary is that other virtue of non-
resistance.   Count Tolstoy in one of his powerful
but unbalanced lay sermons tells us how a learned
Jew, with whom he was discussing, traced every
precept of Christianity back to Hebrew traditions
—except this one precept of non-resistance; and it
is known that Tolstoy himself would build upon
this rock the whole fabric of his reform.   Such
an attitude is doubtless the extravagance of a

fanatical mind and further contains within itself—
as I shall attempt to prove—the mischievous error
of assuming as a universal law what was meant to
be a rule for an elect few. Yet I cannot see how
any candid inquirer can study the words and life
of Christ without acknowledging that the precept
of non-resistance was intended to be taken literally
and absolutely by those to whom it was given.
Blessed are the peace-makers, he says, and blessed
are they which are persecuted for righteousness'
sake. And again, in the same discourse, he
enounces the rule with careful precision: " Resist
not evil; but whosoever shall smite thee on thy
right cheek, turn to him the other also. And if
any man will sue thee at law, and take away thy
coat, let him have thy cloak also." This virtue
of non-resistance is no more than the essential
and inevitable flower of that humility which so
distinguishes Christianity. And throughout those
last days of trial and humiliation the Saviour
never once offered the least resistance to his
persecutors.

Not far removed in character from non-resistance,
and like it consequent on the doctrine of humility,
stands the ideal of perfect poverty. Here at once
we enter upon ground that trenches on socio-
logical questions, and unfortunately no statement
can be made quite so categorical as in the case of
humility and non-resistance. Yet again a candid
consideration of the preaching and example of
Christ must, I think, lead to the conclusion that

he wished his disciples to eschew the possession of all property including even what we should call the necessaries of life. " Where your treasure is, there will your heart be also," he declared, and seemed to feel that the pursuit of the kingdom of heaven was too urgent to admit even the least temporising with the interests of this world; for ye cannot serve God and mammon. So when he sent forth his disciples to preach, he bade them take neither gold nor scrip for their journey, nor two coats. And in the case of the rich young man whom Jesus loved, the last command was to sell all that he had and to separate himself from the world. However repugnant to modern notions this rule of absolute poverty may be, yet it certainly contains an element of real beauty. " Therefore I say unto you, Take no thought for your life, what ye shall eat, or what ye shall drink; nor yet for your body, what ye shall put on;" and thereupon follows that most exquisite parable of the fowls of the air and the lilies of the field, which has lingered on through Christian art and poetry. " Take therefore no thought for the morrow: for the morrow shall take thought for the things of itself. Sufficient unto the day is the evil thereof." And despite the abuses which arose in the begging orders from their pretensions to follow this rule of poverty, the precept did now and then bring forth the highest and purest type of Christian character. Search the annals of the Church and you will find no one who walked

nearer than St. Francis of Assisi to the supreme
model of holy living.   Protestant and Catholic
alike must admit this; and poverty with St.
Francis was a passion no less exigent for spiritual
growth than humility and chastity; and the following of this austere law created in him that same
saintly joy and that same exquisite beauty of sympathy with all sentient beings of which we catch
glimpses in the story of Jesus.

The name of St. Francis brings us to the last
and in some respects most important of those virtues which lie between the aspirations of pure
spirituality and the commands of prohibitive
morality,—I mean the much disputed virtue of
chastity.   I have heard one who was both a man
of the world and a philosopher avow that self-re-
spect and a regard for happiness in the higher
sense of the word might provoke in the heart
every renunciation except this one habit of chastity.   That is merely to say that chastity,
considered as a law which regulates the very
imaginations of the heart, is something more
than a mere prohibition; it is a supplanting of the
earthly life by the desires and aspirations of the
spirit.   There is no doubt that the Church from
a very early age looked upon chastity as the
crowning glory of the religious life; even St. Paul
seems to have regarded it as a desirable, but not
always possible, state for those who dedicated
themselves to holiness.   I am willing to admit,
however, that the position of Christ himself in the

matter is open to some ambiguity. I remember
his action at the marriage feast of Cana, and again
his saying, always so solemnly repeated at mar-
riages to-day: " What therefore God hath joined
together, let not man put asunder." Yet it is
probable that this was no more than a concession
to the world, a hesitancy to push matters spiritual
into regions where they do not belong, the appeal
of charity pleading for the beauty and innocence
of a life which in his austerer moments he resolutely condemned. For herein lies the burning
question of religion and the world. If, as the
deeper voice of inspiration proclaims within us
when the breast is calm, this earthly existence is
a station of groaning and travailling, then the one
purpose of religion is to lift us out of the world
altogether, and the allurement of love is the last
snare to be avoided, the last illusion to be dissi-
pated, the more perilous because of its mask of
beauty. As for Christ it is at least apparent that
he regarded chastity as the simplest and best state
for those who were to be his immediate followers.
He himself did not always abstain from the pleas-
ures of life and men accused him of being a wine-
bibber and a glutton; yet he thought it necessary
for his mission to abjure all family bonds. When
these ties were pressed upon him, he replied
sternly: " Who is my mother? and who are my
brethren?" And to his disciples he said: " If
any man come to me, and hate not his father, and
mother . . . yea, and his own life also, he

cannot be my disciple." So far, however, chastity
may be set down as a mere matter of expediency
more or less urgent upon those who were to give
themselves up to the exigencies of a missionary
career; but it is possible, I think, to go further
than that and to say that Christ looked upon
chastity as the last act of spiritual faith or dominion
in the religious path. His various words on the
relation of the sexes seem to imply this thought
as their deeper content. In one case he is re-
ported to have spoken more explicitly: "There
be eunuchs, which have made themselves eunuchs
for the kingdom of heaven's sake;" and again he
declared that "in the resurrection they neither
marry nor are given in marriage." Such state-
ments as these, though isolated in the Gospels,
when taken with the general tendency of Christ's
teaching and with the wide and early doctrine of
the Church, have considerable weight; and if in
addition to this we consider the experience of men
throughout the world who have sought the inner
sanctuary of holiness, the law may be accepted, I
think, as final.

In these four virtues (or three, if we choose to
omit chastity) is contained the strictly religious
or spiritual teaching of Christ as it bears on the
social aspect of life. The law of love, which
might at first seem to demand inclusion, is in
reality something much deeper and wider than
these social virtues. It is akin to the power of
faith and hope which seizes upon spiritual things;

it is a state of the soul and only by extension is
concerned with our individual life among men.
To reach the source and home of this pure virtue
of love we must, as Emerson wrote, mount above
the bonds of earthly life

> Into vision where all form
> In one only form dissolves;
> In a region where the wheel
> On which all beings ride
> Visibly revolves;
> Where the starred, eternal worm
> Girds the world with bound and term;
> Where unlike things are like;
> Where good and ill,
> And joy and moan,
> Melt into one.

It is, to be sure, this high charity, to use its older
name, that pervades the four religious virtues,
giving them their tone and beauty, and binding
them to the spiritual life; it is the essence even of
the prohibitive law; but it is not specific in any
such sense as humility, poverty, non-resistance,
and chastity are specific.

We may be confirmed in accepting these virtues
as the cardinal doctrine of Christ who to the
Western world stands as the inspired exemplar of
the religious instinct, by turning for a moment
to the great prophet of the Orient. I have not
the desire to examine here in much detail the
Buddhistic doctrine.   Nor is such an examination
necessary; for, whether we regard Buddhism as

the equal or the inferior of Christianity, it at least
has the good fortune of presenting to us in the
Pâli books a more consistent and more amply
logical body of dogma than the Gospels. This is
chiefly due to the fact that Buddhism appeals
more to the reason and less to the emotions than
Christianity.

We may pass over the Buddhistic conception of
faith, hope, and love, with the remark that they
are as essential there as in Christianity, though
of course somewhat different in tone. Nor need
we discuss the prohibitive commands of Buddhism
which are substantially the same as the Jewish.
To his closer followers (who were organised by him
into something like the monastic order) Buddha
taught a system of higher morality which, so far
at least as it bears on social relations, was strikingly like that of Christ.

Humility, to be sure, in the precise Christian
sense of the word cannot be called a Hindu idea;
yet the starting-point of Buddhism depends on a
state of mind not entirely dissimilar to it. Christian humility is associated with a feeling of self-
debasement of the sinful soul standing before a
perfectly righteous judge who rewards and con-
demns as one man judges another. This peculiarly emotional quality Buddhistic renunciation
does not possess, for the simple reason that the
Buddhist acknowledges no personal and eternal
God. But in one respect the two forms of renunciation approach each other. The self-debasement

of the Christian was for the purpose of receiving
finally a crown of glory; it was a putting away
of the lower nature, of the old Adam within the
breast, that the higher nature might grow and, in
accordance with mystic views early developed in
the Church, be absorbed in the perfect holiness of
Christ. Take out of this the relation of the soul
to a personal Saviour, and the Buddhist conception
of humility, or self-abnegation, is obtained. In one
of the Pâli books Buddha distinguishes between
the cravings of the lower and higher natures
in a manner that throws light on this similarity.

There[1] are two cravings, O priests; the noble one,
and the ignoble one. And what, O priests, is the ignoble
craving? We may have, O priests, the case of one who,
himself subject to birth, craves what is subject to birth;
himself subject to old age, craves what is subject to old
age; himself subject to disease, . . . death, . . .
sorrow, . . . corruption, . . . craves what is
subject to corruption. . . . And what, O priests,
is the noble craving? We may have, O priests, the case
of one who, himself subject to birth, perceives the
wretchedness of what is subject to birth, and craves the
incomparable security of a Nirvana free from birth;
himself subject to old age, . . . disease, . . .
death, . . . sorrow, . . . corruption, perceives the
wretchedness of what is subject to corruption, and craves
the incomparable security of a Nirvana free from corruption.

Here lies the gist of the matter. The fashion
of this world passeth away; what is born must

[1] Translated by Henry C. Warren.

perish; all things are impermanent, and most impermanent of all is that peculiar combination of desires and repulsions which we call a man's personal soul. He who would obtain salvation, according to Hindu ideas, must deliberately put away the personal self and look for a state of peace and deliverance surpassing in joy the conception of heavenly rewards:

> The strong gods pine for my abode,
>   And pine in vain the sacred Seven;
> But thou, meek lover of the good!
>   Find me, and turn thy back on heaven.

It is unfortunate (for us at least of the Western world who would approach Buddhism intelligently) that the name of this condition of salvation, the word "Nirvana," should contain only the negative idea of the snuffing out of the lower cravings as a candle flame is blown out, and should omit the positive idea of joy which for the true Buddhist this state signifies. If the word is negative, that is merely because the positive aspect of deliverance cannot be expressed in rational language. The identity of Nirvana with nihilism is a fatuity strongly condemned by Buddha himself. In relation to the higher craving of the heart this self-abnegation of the Buddhist is then not unlike Christian humility. Nor is its bearing on the social life of man much different from that of its Christian congener; they both lead to a contempt for the conflict of worldly

16

ambitions, and to a certain self-withdrawal before the impertinent demands of society.

It is easy therefore to see how the virtues following such a guidance should be ascetic in their nature. Non-resistance in Buddhism was extended to the forbidding of all violence whatsoever, and life even of the lowest orders was held sacred. There are many stories in the Pâli books setting forth the beauty of absolute submission to violence and malice. One well-known stanza in which the idea of non-resistance is fully expressed, it may not be amiss to quote here. " ' He has abused me, he has struck me, he has oppressed me, he has robbed me,'—those who harbour such thoughts fail to put an end to enmity. ' He has abused me, he has struck me, he has oppressed me, he has robbed me,'—those who do not harbour such thoughts, they put an end to enmity." Strict poverty also was enjoined. The disciple was allowed only eight possessions: an alms-bowl, razor, needle, belt, water-strainer, and three robes. Neither the community nor the individual monk could own money, and food was obtained only by begging. Absolute chastity was prescribed, and all family ties were severed in order that no impediment might remain in the path of enlightenment.

Despite some difference of emotional tone the religious codes of Christ and Buddha, as they touch on vital social questions, are thus seen to be in unison; and where these two leaders of the

West and of the East agree so perfectly, I am content to believe that the religious instinct has been voiced in its greatest purity. What then shall we say to those who in the specific gospel of Christ seek to find a law that shall supplant the long-established laws of society? Or to those who hear in the warning voice of the religious instinct a power that shall set some theory of humanitarian equality in place of the old evolutional reign of competition? The doctrines of Christ if accepted by the world in their integrity,— the virtues, that is, of humility, non-resistance, and poverty,—would not institute any such desired revolution in society; they would simply make an end of the whole social fabric; and if to these chastity be added, they would do away with human existence altogether. As a matter of fact Christ, according to the overwhelming evidence of the Gospels, never for a moment contemplated the introduction of a religion which should rebuild society. His kingdom was not of this world, and there is every reason to believe that he looked to see only a few chosen souls follow in his footsteps. He declares of himself that he was sent only to the lost sheep of the house of Israel; and when he sent forth the twelve, he commanded them to go not into the way of the Gentiles and not to enter any city of the Samaritans. The world at large was to him a wicked and adulterous generation, moving toward the consummation of its sin; " for wide is the gate, and broad is the way, that leadeth to destruction, and many there be which go in thereat." Out of this habitation of wickedness he called his disciples to leave their nets or their seat at the receipt of custom, and to abandon (if necessary even to hate) father and mother and every earthly tie; they were to leave all and make themselves ready for the kingdom of heaven. We are told, you reply, that he bade his disciples to go into all the world and preach the Gospel. This is true, but the words are so manifestly in disaccord with the whole tenor of Christ's life and teaching that the passage may be strongly suspected to be of later origin. And, granting that the words are authentic, they still detract nothing from the present argument; for in the Gospel of Matthew where the same command is repeated there follows immediately that lurid account of the sin and desolation of the world whose ruin is only delayed until the unheeded Gospel has been carried abroad. Although this particular picture of the final catastrophe is in the record inextricably confused with an *ex-post-facto* prophecy of the fall of Jerusalem, yet there can be little doubt, from tradition and from the early and universal belief of the Church, that Christ looked for the speedy destruction of the world. Out of the consummation of wickedness which was to call down a general curse on the race, some few faithful believers, like Noah and his family at the time of the Flood, were to be saved and gathered into the kingdom of heaven. The prophecy is quite clear, however much prejudice may have sought to pervert its meaning: " Verily I say unto you, That there be some of them that stand here, which shall not taste of death, till they have seen the kingdom of God come into power." He nowhere intimates that the law and custom of the world can be changed; he accepts these things as necessary to the social system. He rebukes the Pharisees for their hypocrisy in religion, but never speaks against the power of civil authority. " Ye know," he says, " that they which are accounted to rule over the Gentiles exercise lordship over them; and their great ones exercise authority upon them. But so shall it not be among you: but whosoever will be great among you, shall be your minister (*i. e.*, servant)." Not a word falls from his lips to indicate that slavery should be abolished, or the hierarchy of government disturbed. When the disciples question him about the paying of taxes, he bids them pay what is demanded, not because they themselves are in any way a part of the civil order, but because he is unwilling to give offence. And again when tempted by the Pharisees he replies in those ringing words: " Render to Cæsar the things that are Cæsar's, and to God the things that are God's." There is something of peculiar pathos in the story of the rich young man whom Jesus loved and to whom he pointed out more clearly than to any other this fixed gulf between the ideals of the world and of religion. All the virtues of the world the zealous inquirer had observed, yet one thing was wanting; and still to-day as we read the story we can almost hear the reluctance and pity in Jesus' voice, as he bade the young man look to another and sterner law of renunciation if he would be perfect. The gist of the whole matter is contained in those two pithy sayings: My kingdom is not of this world, and, Ye cannot serve God and mammon.

In this point again we find Buddhism and Christianity in accord, except that what is expressed in the Gospels more or less vaguely is in the Pâli books ordained with rigorous precision. The believers in India were divided into two distinct classes: those who formed the *saṅga*, or church properly speaking, and who, looking to Nirvana as their goal, accepted the religious life as we have described it; and those who acknowledged the higher ideal but chose rather to seek their reward in a heaven of prolonged but not eternal happiness. These latter remained in the world as merchants or soldiers or rulers, and their adherence to the faith was particularly marked by *dâna*, or liberal giving,—a virtue of supreme importance where the true disciples depended entirely on charity for their support. Buddha, even more clearly than Christ, recognised and taught the evil and insufficiency of human society; and he saw also, as did Christ, that the religious instinct, if followed out, must result in the utter abrogation of that society and not in any practical alteration of its laws.

Yet because the religious inspiration and virtues avert their face from this world, it does not follow that the law of competition reigns among men without restriction or alleviation, or that human society is left wholly to the ravening of wolfish and tigerish desires. The world has its code of ethics as well as the spirit. First of all the prohibitive commands are universally binding: Thou shalt not kill, Thou shalt not steal, etc. And far above these stands the guiding principle of character, corresponding to the aspiration of the spirit but concerned with that lower personality which buys and sells, marries and gives in marriage, and looks to earthly success as its reward. And this principle of character shows itself under three manifestations in the same way as the law of the spirit. As faith is the act of discriminating between the things of the body and the things of the spirit, so prudence, or worldly wisdom, (the Platonic σοφία would better convey the meaning,) is the faculty of discerning the relative values of the things of this earth. As hope is the joy and persistence of faith, so courage is that which leads a man to follow diligently the dictates of prudence; it is the joy and strength of secular activity, for no man without courage ever won the prize of success, or winning it held it in gladness. And as love is the flower of faith and hope, the faculty of the spirit that reaches down and gives vitality to the religious virtues, so honour is the flower of prudence and courage, the guiding principle through the intricate demands of worldly uprightness.

Now these three — prudence, courage, and honour,—like their spiritual congeners, are not specific virtues touching the relation of man to man, but affect rather the integrity of a man's character itself. Between these and the prohibitive commands lie the social virtues of the secular life, which are curiously similar to the religious virtues, yet perfectly distinct from them. In place of humility, or self-abnegation, which abjures the desires and contentions of life altogether, stands justice in its stricter acceptance,— justice which implies the wish to attain for oneself and to allow to all others what the ability and energy and industry of each merit. For non-resistance we have the civil virtue of mercy, which does not abrogate justice or claim for the weak what is due to the strong, but softens its asperities by recognising that after all human judgment is liable to err and that where doubts arise it is magnanimous to surrender somewhat to the less fortunate. It is, strictly considered, an extension of justice as nonresistance is an extension of humility. So in place of poverty we should have charity in its limited sense of liberal giving; and in place of chastity, temperance and faithfulness. These four—justice, mercy, charity, and temperance— are positive in their effect and supplement the mere prohibitions of universal morality; but they are not religious and they do not spring from the religious instinct, neither do they in any sense controvert, however much they may mitigate, the law of competition which governs the material world.

> By right or wrong,
> Lands and goods go to the strong.
> Property will brutely draw
> Still to the proprietor;
> Silver to silver creep and wind,
> And kind to kind.

They are, in brief, the logical working out of that precept of Apollo, *Nothing too much*, which as developed by Aristotle and others has always been and must always remain the acting rule of human society. If, in distinction to this command of Apollo, we should wish to express briefly the ideal of religious virtue, we could not do better than repeat the words of the *Imitation :* " Tene breve et consummatum verbum: Dimitte omnia, et invenies omnia; relinque cupidinem, et reperies requiem,"—Put away all things and thou shalt find all things, abandon desire and thou shalt attain peace.

If you ask whence arises the widespread belief that the old order of things is to pass away and a new reign of humanitarianism to be introduced, the answer is ready to hand: it arises from that inexhaustible source of error, the failure to discern distinctions. It is the good fortune of Mr. Mallock to have set forth the nature of this

confusion of socialistic ideas in the economic field.
He has discriminated clearly between the phenomena of social aggregates considered as wholes
on the one hand, and on the other hand the problems which arise out of the conflict of different
parts within these aggregates. The progress of
mankind as a race is the slow process of evolution
caused by the survival of the fittest; the rapid
progress of any particular aggregate is due to the
directive activity of the "great men" within that
aggregate working through the law of competition. Justice and the general welfare demand
that the "great man" receive his proper material
reward. The introduction of the idea of humanity
as a whole into problems of this second order has
brought about the wild and mischievous notions
of humanitarian economy now so prevalent. The
laws of society are fixed, and no amount of senti-
mental yearning will alter their nature; although
it may very well create infinite distrust and class-
hatred.

The religious ground of humanitarianism is a
like failure to observe distinctions,—a failure here
to discriminate between the ideals of religion and
the ideals of the world. To apply the laws of the
spirit to the activities of this earth is at once a
desecration and denial of religion and a bewildering and unsettling of the social order. To intrude
the aspirations of faith and hope and the ethics of
the golden rule of love into regions where prudence
and courage and the dictates of honour are su-

preme, is a mischievous folly. Failure to discriminate between the virtues that spring from these ideals, or any attempt to amalgamate the religious virtues and the secular virtues, to confuse humility with justice, non-resistance with mercy, poverty with liberality, chastity with temperance,—such blindness is equally absurd and vastly more dangerous. Humanitarianism is just this vague sentimentality of a mind that refuses to distinguish between the golden rule and the precept of Apollo. There are gross and manifest evils in the actual working of the law of competition, no one denies that. But they are to be set right, if right is possible in this world, by a clearer understanding and a more faithful observance of the worldly virtues, and not by the sickly yearnings of sentimentalists. It is still well that we render to Cæsar the things that are Cæsar's and to God the things that are God's.

For society at large the problem is an easy one; society as a whole has nothing to do with God and everything to do with Cæsar. Indeed, as the economic fallacy of socialism springs from applying the laws of humanity as a whole to any particular aggregate of men; so the religious fallacy is an application of the problem of the individual to such an aggregate of men. But for the individual, in whose heart the religious instinct murmurs and to whom at the same time the voice of the world may speak with equal weight, the question is not always so simple. When faith

was strong among men, as it was for example in
the days of St. Francis, he found it not difficult
perhaps to walk bravely in his chosen path.   Society was divided pretty sharply into those who
followed the law of renunciation and those who
followed the law of ambition, and any attempt to
confuse these two laws would have awakened dis-
quiet and condemnation.   So it was that for St.
Francis himself, when the vision of peace came,
it was not so hard, we may suppose, to see his
way perfectly clear before him.   But in other
days when faith grows a little dull and the all-
levelling power of democracy has brought things
spiritual and things worldly to the same plane,—
or so at least it looks to the eyes of men,—in such
days the path of the individual is beset with difficulties.   The man of the world is troubled at
times by a voice that calls upon him to renounce:
and on the other side it is still harder, if not impossible, to follow the religious life in its simplicity
and purity.   What shall be said to the troubled
soul in whose confused hearing the voices of the
world and the spirit are mingled, dragging him
now this way and now that?   I know not unless
it be in the quaint metaphor of Emerson, which I
have already quoted in an earlier essay:

One key, one solution to the mysteries of human
condition, one solution to the old knots of fate, freedom
and foreknowledge, exists, the propounding, namely, of
the double consciousness.   A man must ride alternately
on the horses of his private and his public nature, as the

equestrians in the circus throw themselves nimbly from horse to horse, or plant one foot on the back of one and the other foot on the back of the other.

Such a double life he must lead, balancing between the two laws, but above all things taking care not to confuse the regions in which these laws are valid or to lose the distinction between his public and his private duty. To lose such a distinction is to fall forthwith into the shadows of hypocrisy and charlatanry; to maintain it ever before the inner eye and to judge honestly between the conflict of claims is the great problem which is left to the conscience of each man and to him alone.

THE END

HOUSTON PUBLIC LIBRARY
CENTRAL LIBRARY

This book may be kept for FOURTEEN DAYS.
With due notice, it may be renewed once
for the same period. A charge is made for
overdue books.

S-4-69-50M-1